Weather and Climate Inventory
National Park Service
San Francisco Bay Area Network

Natural Resource Technical Report NPS/SFAN/NRTR—2007/041
WRCC Report 2007-16

Christopher A. Davey, Kelly T. Redmond, and David B. Simeral
Western Regional Climate Center
Desert Research Institute
2215 Raggio Parkway
Reno, Nevada 89512-1095

May 2007

U.S. Department of the Interior
National Park Service
Natural Resource Program Center
Fort Collins, Colorado

The Natural Resource Publication series addresses natural resource topics that are of interest and applicability to a broad readership in the National Park Service and to others in the management of natural resources, including the scientific community, the public, and the National Park Service conservation and environmental constituencies. Manuscripts are peer-reviewed to ensure that the information is scientifically credible, technically accurate, appropriately written for the intended audience, and designed and published in a professional manner.

The Natural Resources Technical Reports series is used to disseminate the peer-reviewed results of scientific studies in the physical, biological, and social sciences for both the advancement of science and the achievement of the National Park Service mission. The reports provide contributors with a forum for displaying comprehensive data that are often deleted from journals because of page limitations. Current examples of such reports include the results of research that address natural resource management issues; natural resource inventory and monitoring activities; resource assessment reports; scientific literature reviews; and peer-reviewed proceedings of technical workshops, conferences, or symposia.

Views and conclusions in this report are those of the authors and do not necessarily reflect policies of the National Park Service. Mention of trade names or commercial products does not constitute endorsement or recommendation for use by the National Park Service.

Printed copies of reports in these series may be produced in a limited quantity and they are only available as long as the supply lasts. This report is also available from the Natural Resource Publications Management website (http://www.nature.nps.gov/publications/NRPM) on the Internet or by sending a request to the address on the back cover.

Please cite this publication as follows:

Davey, C. A., K. T. Redmond, and D. B. Simeral. 2007. Weather and Climate Inventory, National Park Service, San Francisco Bay Area Network. Natural Resource Technical Report NPS/SFAN/NRTR—2007/041. National Park Service, Fort Collins, Colorado.

NPS/SFAN/NRTR—2007/041, May 2007

Contents

Contents (continued)

Figures

Tables

Appendixes

Acronyms

AASC	American Association of State Climatologists
ACIS	Applied Climate Information System
ASOS	Automated Surface Observing System
AWOS	Automated Weather Observing System
BAMI	Bay Area Mesoscale Initiative
BLM	Bureau of Land Management
CARB	California Air Resources Board
CASTNet	Clean Air Status and Trends Network
CIMIS	California Irrigation Management Information System
COOP	Cooperative Observer Program
CRN	Climate Reference Network
CWOP	Citizen Weather Observer Program
DFIR	Double-Fence Intercomparison Reference
DRI	Desert Research Institute
DST	daylight savings time
ENSO	El Niño Southern Oscillation
EUON	Eugene O'Neill National Historic Site
EPA	Environmental Protection Agency
FAA	Federal Aviation Administration
FIPS	Federal Information Processing Standards
FOPO	Fort Point National Historic Site
GMT	Greenwich Mean Time
GOES	Geostationary Operational Environmental Satellite
GOGA	Golden Gate National Recreation Area
GPMP	NPS Gaseous Pollutant Monitoring Program
GPS	Global Positioning System
GPS-MET	NOAA ground-based GPS meteorology
I&M	NPS Inventory and Monitoring Program
JOMU	John Muir National Historic Site
LEO	Low Earth Orbit
LST	local standard time
MUWO	Muir Woods National Monument
MDN	Mercury Deposition Network
NADP	National Atmospheric Deposition Program
NASA	National Aeronautics and Space Administration
NCDC	National Climatic Data Center
NetCDF	Network Common Data Form
NOAA	National Oceanic and Atmospheric Administration
NPS	National Park Service
NRCS	Natural Resources Conservation Service
NWS	National Weather Service
PDO	Pacific Decadal Oscillation
PINN	Pinnacles National Monument
PNA	Pacific-North America Oscillation

PORE	Point Reyes National Seashore
PRISM	Parameter Regression on Independent Slopes Model
PRSF	Presidio of San Francisco
RAWS	Remote Automated Weather Station network
RCC	regional climate center
SAO	Surface Airways Observation network
SFAN	San Francisco Bay Area Inventory and Monitoring Network
SOD	Summary Of the Day
Surfrad	Surface Radiation Budget network
SNOTEL	Snowfall Telemetry network
USDA	U.S. Department of Agriculture
USGS	U.S. Geological Survey
UTC	Coordinated Universal Time
WBAN	Weather Bureau Army Navy
WMO	World Meteorological Organization
WRCC	Western Regional Climate Center
WX4U	Weather For You network

Executive Summary

Climate is a dominant factor driving the physical and ecologic processes affecting the San Francisco Bay Area Inventory and Monitoring Network (SFAN). Knowledge about weather and climate is critical because they affect not just geophysical and biological resources but ecosystem drivers and processes. Key reasons for monitoring weather and climate in network parks are because the effects can be long-lasting on (1) plant and animal populations, some of which are listed as endangered or threatened species, (2) on air and water quality, and (3) on drought and flood cycles, fires, mass wasting and other catastrophic events. Long-term weather data can also contribute to the understanding of global climate change and its effects on SFAN ecosystems. Because of its influence on the ecology of SFAN park units, climate was identified as a high-priority vital sign for SFAN and is one of the 12 basic inventories to be completed for all National Park Service (NPS) Inventory and Monitoring Program (I&M) networks.

This project was initiated to inventory past and present climate monitoring efforts in the SFAN. In this report, we provide the following information:

- Overview of broad-scale climatic factors and zones important to SFAN park units.
- Inventory of weather and climate station locations in and near SFAN park units relevant to the NPS I&M Program.
- Results of an inventory of metadata on each weather station, including affiliations for weather-monitoring networks, types of measurements recorded at these stations, and information about the actual measurements (length of record, etc.).
- Initial evaluation of the adequacy of coverage for existing weather stations and recommendations for improvements in monitoring weather and climate.

Rugged topography and proximity to the Pacific Ocean work together to create exceptionally severe climatic gradients in SFAN park units. The Mediterranean-style climate of the SFAN is generally typified by cool, wet winters and warm, dry summers, with greater annual temperature variations inland compared to the coast. Mean annual precipitation for the SFAN is greatest for the park units along the coast, including Golden Gate National Recreation Area (GOGA), Muir Woods National Monument (MUWO), and Point Reyes National Seashore (PORE). These areas generally receive over 1000 mm of precipitation each year. In contrast, Pinnacles National Monument (PINN) generally receives less than 500 mm of precipitation each year. Mean annual temperatures across the SFAN exhibit sharp coast-interior gradients and range from 12°C at PORE to over 14°C for John Muir National Historic Site (JOMU) and PINN. During the winter months, minimum temperatures are often above 5°C along the coast but drop below 0°C in PINN. Summer maximum temperatures are well below 20°C for the coastal park units but often exceed 35°C in the warmest park units, like PINN. The El Niño Southern Oscillation (ENSO), Pacific Decadal Oscillation (PDO), and Pacific-North America Oscillation (PNA) all influence intra- and inter-annual climate variability in the SFAN.

Through a search of national databases and inquiries to NPS staff, we have identified 31 weather and climate stations within SFAN park units. GOGA has the most stations within park boundaries (13). Most of the weather and climate stations identified for SFAN park units had metadata and data records that are sufficiently complete and satisfactory in quality.

The SFAN network recognizes the continuing need for improved weather and climate station coverage within its park units. Weather and climate monitoring efforts at SFAN are already planning to maintain or establish several different types of climate and precipitation monitoring stations. Some of the SFAN park units do not currently host any weather or climate stations and must therefore rely on outside data sources. These include Eugene O'Neill National Historic Site (EUON), Fort Point National Historic Site (FOPO), JOMU, and Presidio of San Francisco (PRSF). Fortunately, many outside data sources are available in SFAN's largely urban setting. These outside sources are also important as there are no reliable sources for long-term climate records for the SFAN park units in the San Francisco Bay Area. The long-term COOP (Cooperative Observer Program) stations that we did identify in PORE (Point Reyes Light Stn.) and GOGA (Mount Tamalpais 2 SW) do not have reliable data records.

Many of the notable outside sources of climate data, such as the COOP station "San Francisco," have experienced heavy urbanization during their periods of record. These urbanization influences will tend to obscure any background signals of global-scale temperature changes. Those SFAN park units containing more pristine locations for monitoring climate changes (e.g., PORE) do not have reliable long-term records.

In addition to defining long-term climate characteristics and trends across the SFAN, and their impacts on SFAN ecosystems, the network is also interested in documenting the characteristics of extreme weather/climate conditions. The significant topographical variations and severe coastal-interior gradients that are present in many SFAN parks means that many of the more extreme characteristics of SFAN climate can only be detected at smaller spatial scales. Very dense weather and climate station coverage would be necessary to sample adequately the local-scale variations in temperature and precipitation that are present in the SFAN, especially near the coast in park units like GOGA and PORE. However, large areas of both parks remain unsampled (e.g., northernmost PORE; coastal sections of PORE along Drakes Bay, Point Lobos in GOGA). Installing new weather stations in areas such as these would be of immediate benefit for SFAN climate monitoring efforts.

Most of the weather and climate stations we identified in PINN are located in the central part of the park unit, concentrated primarily near the east entrance and the Bear Gulch Visitor Center. Much of northern and southern PINN remains unsampled. We acknowledge that these areas within PINN are relatively remote, with no road access points. However, climate monitoring efforts in PINN, particularly those efforts related to better understanding spatial temperature and precipitation variations in the park unit, would benefit greatly by targeting these unsampled areas with new stations. Initially, a near-real-time station could be considered for the west entrance or at Chaparral Ranger Station, as the west side of PINN does not appear to be sampled currently by any weather or climate stations.

Acknowledgements

This work was supported and completed under Task Agreement H8R07010001, with the Great Basin Cooperative Ecosystem Studies Unit. We would like to acknowledge very helpful assistance from various National Park Service personnel associated with the San Francisco Bay Area Inventory and Monitoring Network. Particular thanks are extended to Marcus Koenen and Paul Johnson. We also thank John Gross, Margaret Beer, Grant Kelly, Greg McCurdy, and Heather Angeloff for all their help. Seth Gutman with the National Oceanic and Atmospheric Administration Earth Systems Research Laboratory provided valuable input on the GPS-MET station network. Portions of the work were supported by the NOAA Western Regional Climate Center.

1.0. Introduction

Weather and climate are key drivers in ecosystem structure and function. Global- and regional-scale climate variations will have a tremendous impact on natural systems (Chapin et al. 1996; Schlesinger 1997; Jacobson et al. 2000; Bonan 2002). Long-term patterns in temperature and precipitation provide first-order constraints on potential ecosystem structure and function. Secondary constraints are realized from the intensity and duration of individual weather events and, additionally, from seasonality and inter-annual climate variability. These constraints influence the fundamental properties of ecologic systems, such as soil–water relationships, plant–soil processes, and nutrient cycling, as well as disturbance rates and intensity. These properties, in turn, influence the life-history strategies supported by a climatic regime (Neilson 1987; Rodriguez-Iturbe 2000; NPS 2005).

Given the importance of climate, it is one of 12 basic inventories to be completed by the National Park Service (NPS) Inventory and Monitoring Program (I&M) network (I&M 2006). As primary environmental drivers for the other vital signs, weather and climate patterns present various practical and management consequences and implications for the NPS (Oakley et al. 2003). Most park units observe weather and climate elements as part of their overall mission. The lands under NPS stewardship provide many excellent locations for monitoring climatic conditions.

It is essential that park units within the San Francisco Bay Area Inventory and Monitoring Network (SFAN) have an effective climate-monitoring system in place to track climate changes and to aid in management decisions relating to these changes. The purpose of this report is to determine the current status of weather and climate monitoring within the SFAN (Table 1.1; Figure 1.1). In this report, we provide the following informational elements:

- Overview of broad-scale climatic factors and zones important to SFAN park units.
- Inventory of locations for all weather stations in and near SFAN park units that are relevant to the NPS I&M networks.
- Results of metadata inventory for each station, including weather-monitoring network affiliations, types of recorded measurements, and information about actual measurements (length of record, etc.).
- Initial evaluation of the adequacy of coverage for existing weather stations and recommendations for improvements in monitoring weather and climate.

The primary objectives for climate- and weather-monitoring activities in SFAN are as follows (NPS 2005):

A. Determine variability and long-term trends in climate through monthly and annual summaries of selected weather parameters (temperature and precipitation).
B. Identify and determine frequencies and patterns of extreme climatic conditions for common weather parameters.
C. Determine the impact of climate changes on biotic and abiotic resources.

1.1. Network Terminology

Before proceeding, it is important to stress that this report discusses the idea of "networks" in two different ways. Modifiers are used to distinguish between NPS I&M networks and weather/climate station networks. See Appendix A for a full definition of these terms.

Table 1.1. Park units in the San Francisco Bay Area Network.

Acronym	Name
EUON	Eugene O'Neill National Historic Site
FOPO	Fort Point National Historic Site
GOGA	Golden Gate National Recreation Area
JOMU	John Muir National Historic Site
MUWO	Muir Woods National Monument
PINN	Pinnacles National Monument
PORE	Point Reyes National Seashore
PRSF	Presidio of San Francisco

1.1.1. Weather and Climate Station Networks

Most weather and climate measurements are made not from isolated stations but from stations that are part of a network operated in support of a particular mission. The limiting case is a network of one station, where measurements are made by an interested observer or group. Larger networks usually have additional inventory data and station-tracking procedures. Some national weather and climate networks are associated with the National Oceanic and Atmospheric Administration (NOAA), including the National Weather Service (NWS) Cooperative Observer Program (COOP). Other national networks include the interagency Remote Automated Weather Station network (RAWS) and the U.S. Department of Agriculture/Natural Resources Conservation Service (USDA/NRCS) Snowfall Telemetry (SNOTEL) and snowcourse networks. Usually a single agency, but sometimes a consortium of interested parties, will jointly support a particular weather/climate network.

1.1.2. NPS I&M Networks

Within the NPS, the system for monitoring various attributes in the participating park units (about 270–280 in total) is divided into 32 NPS I&M networks. These networks are collections of park units grouped together around a common theme, typically geographical.

1.2. Weather versus Climate Definitions

It is also important to distinguish whether the primary use of a given station is for weather purposes or for climate purposes. Weather station networks are intended for near-real-time usage, where the precise circumstances of a set of measurements are typically less important. In these cases, changes in exposure or other attributes over time are not as critical. Climate networks, however, are intended for long-term tracking of atmospheric conditions. Siting and exposure are critical factors for climate networks, and it is vitally important that the observational circumstances remain essentially unchanged over the duration of the station record.

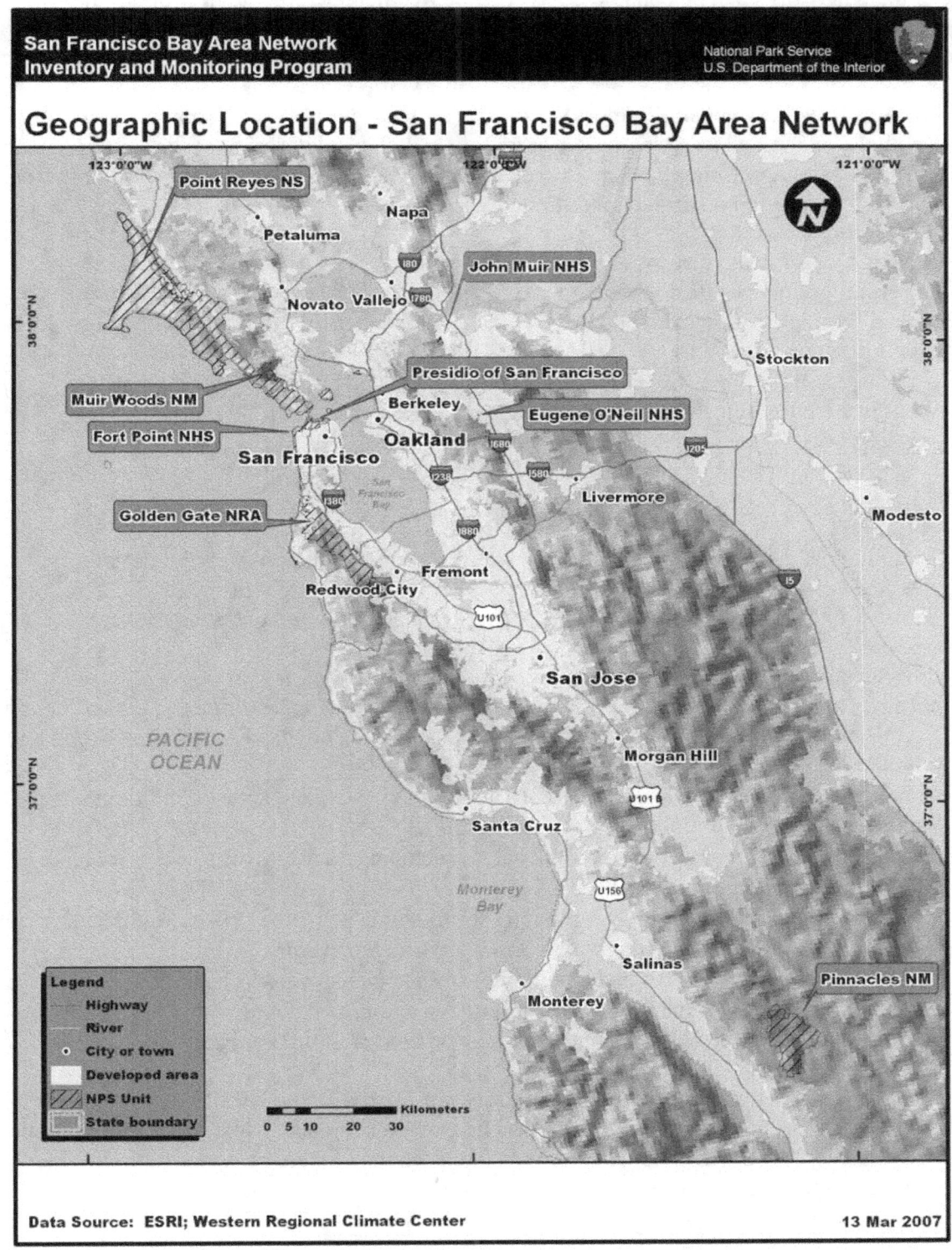

Figure 1.1. Map of the San Francisco Bay Area Network.

Some climate networks can be considered hybrids of weather and climate networks. These hybrid climate networks can supply information on a short-term "weather" time scale and a longer-term "climate" time scale.

In this report, "weather" generally refers to current (or near-real-time) atmospheric conditions, while "climate" is defined as the complete ensemble of statistical descriptors for temporal and spatial properties of atmospheric behavior (see Appendix A). Climate and weather phenomena shade gradually into each other and are ultimately inseparable.

1.3. Purpose of Measurements

Climate inventory and monitoring climate activities should be based on a set of guiding fundamental principles. Any evaluation of weather/climate monitoring programs begins with asking the following question:

- What is the purpose of weather and climate measurements?

Evaluation of past, present, or planned weather/climate monitoring activities must be based on the answer to this question.

Weather and climate data and information constitute a prominent and widely requested component of the NPS I&M networks (I&M 2006). Within the context of the NPS, the following services constitute the main purposes for recording weather and climate observations:

- Provide measurements for real-time operational needs and early warnings of potential hazards (landslides, mudflows, washouts, fallen trees, plowing activities, fire conditions, aircraft and watercraft conditions, road conditions, rescue conditions, fog, restoration and remediation activities, etc.).
- Provide visitor education and aid interpretation of expected and actual conditions for visitors while they are in the park and for deciding if and when to visit the park.
- Establish engineering and design criteria for structures, roads, culverts, etc., for human comfort, safety, and economic needs.
- Consistently monitor climate over the long-term to detect changes in environmental drivers affecting ecosystems, including both gradual and sudden events.
- Provide retrospective data to understand *a posteriori* changes in flora and fauna.
- Document for posterity the physical conditions in and near the park units, including mean, extreme, and variable measurements (in time and space) for all applications.

The last three items in the preceding list are pertinent primarily to the NPS I&M networks; however, all items are important to NPS operations and management. Most of the needs in this list overlap heavily. It is often impractical to operate separate climate measuring systems that also cannot be used to meet ordinary weather needs, where there is greater emphasis on timeliness and reliability.

1.4. Design of Climate-Monitoring Programs

Determining the purposes for collecting measurements in a given weather/climate monitoring program will guide the process of identifying weather and climate stations suitable for the monitoring program. The context for making these decisions is provided in Chapter 2 where background on the SFAN climate is presented. However, this process is only one step in evaluating and designing a climate-monitoring program. The following steps must also be included:

- Define park and network-specific monitoring needs and objectives.
- Identify locations and data repositories of existing and historic stations.
- Acquire existing data when necessary or practical.
- Evaluate the quality of existing data.
- Evaluate the adequacy of coverage of existing stations.
- Develop a protocol for monitoring the weather and climate, including the following:
  o Standardized summaries and reports of weather/climate data.
  o Data management (quality assurance and quality control, archiving, data access, etc.).
- Develop and implement a plan for installing or modifying stations, as necessary.

Throughout the design process, there are various factors that require consideration in evaluating weather and climate measurements. Many of these factors have been summarized by Dr. Tom Karl, director of the NOAA National Climatic Data Center (NCDC), and widely distributed as the "Ten Principles for Climate Monitoring" (Karl et al. 1996; NRC 2001). These principles are presented in Appendix B, and the guidelines are embodied in many of the comments made throughout this report. The most critical factors are presented here. In addition, an overview of requirements necessary to operate a climate network is provided in Appendix C, with further discussion in Appendix D.

1.4.1. Need for Consistency

A principal goal in climate monitoring is to detect and characterize slow and sudden changes in climate through time. This is of less concern for day-to-day weather changes, but it is of paramount importance for climate variability and change. There are many ways whereby changes in techniques for making measurements, changes in instruments or their exposures, or seemingly innocuous changes in site characteristics can lead to apparent changes in climate. Safeguards must be in place to avoid these false sources of temporal "climate" variability if we are to draw correct inferences about climate behavior over time from archived measurements.

For climate monitoring, consistency through time is vital, counting at least as important as absolute accuracy. Sensors record only what is occurring at the sensor—this is all they can detect. It is the responsibility of station or station network managers to ensure that observations are representative of the spatial and temporal climate scales that we wish to record.

1.4.2. Metadata

Changes in instruments, site characteristics, and observing methodologies can lead to apparent changes in climate through time. It is therefore vital to document all factors that can bear on the interpretation of climate measurements and to update the information repeatedly through time. This information ("metadata," data about data) has its own history and set of quality-control issues that parallel those of the actual data. There is no single standard for the content of climate metadata, but a simple rule suffices:

- Observers should record all information that could be needed in the future to interpret observations correctly without benefit of the observers' personal recollections.

Such documentation includes notes, drawings, site forms, and photos, which can be of inestimable value if taken in the correct manner. That stated, it is not always clear to the metadata provider *what is important* for posterity and *what will be important* in the future. It is almost impossible to "over document" a station. Station documentation is greatly underappreciated and is seldom thorough enough (especially for climate purposes). Insufficient attention to this issue often lowers the present and especially future value of otherwise useful data.

The convention followed throughout climatology is to refer to metadata as information about the measurement process, station circumstances, and data. The term "data" is reserved solely for the actual weather and climate records obtained from sensors.

1.4.3. Maintenance

Inattention to maintenance is the greatest source of failure in weather and climate stations and networks. Problems begin to occur soon after sites are deployed. A regular visit schedule must be implemented, where sites, settings (e.g., vegetation), sensors, communications, and data flow are checked routinely (once or twice a year at a minimum) and updated as necessary. Parts must be changed out for periodic recalibration or replacement. With adequate maintenance, the entire instrument suite should be replaced or completely refurbished about once every five to seven years.

Simple preventive maintenance is effective but requires much planning and skilled technical staff. Changes in technology and products require retraining and continual re-education. Travel, logistics, scheduling, and seasonal access restrictions consume major amounts of time and budget but are absolutely necessary. Without such attention, data gradually become less credible and then often are misused or not used at all.

1.4.4. Automated versus Manual Stations

Historic stations often have depended on manual observations and many continue to operate in this mode. Manual observations frequently produce excellent data sets. Sensors and data are simple and intuitive, well tested, and relatively cheap. Manual stations have much to offer in certain circumstances and can be a source of both primary and backup data. However, methodical consistency for manual measurements is a constant challenge, especially with a mobile work force. Operating manual stations takes time and needs to be done on a regular schedule, though sometimes the routine is welcome.

Nearly all newer stations are automated. Automated stations provide better time resolution, increased (though imperfect) reliability, greater capacity for data storage, and improved accessibility to large amounts of data. The purchase cost for automated stations is higher than for manual stations. A common expectation and serious misconception is that an automated station can be deployed and left to operate on its own. In reality, automation does not eliminate the need for people but rather changes the type of person that is needed. Skilled technical personnel are needed and must be readily available, especially if live communications exist and data gaps are not wanted. Site visits are needed at least annually and spare parts must be maintained. Typical annual costs for sensors and maintenance are $1500–2500 per station per year but these costs still can vary greatly depending on the kind of automated site.

1.4.5. Communications

With manual stations, the observer is responsible for recording and transmitting station data. Data from automated stations, however, can be transmitted quickly for access by research and operations personnel, which is a highly preferable situation. A comparison of communication systems for automated and manual stations shows that automated stations generally require additional equipment, more power, higher transmission costs, attention to sources of disruption or garbling, and backup procedures (e.g., manual downloads from data loggers).

Automated stations are capable of functioning normally without communication and retaining many months of data. At such sites, however, alerts about station problems are not possible, large gaps can accrue when accessible stations quit, and the constituencies needed to support such stations are smaller and less vocal. Two-way communications permit full recovery from disruptions, ability to reprogram data loggers remotely, and better opportunities for diagnostics and troubleshooting. In virtually all cases, two-way communications are much preferred to all other communication methods. However, two-way communications require considerations of cost, signal access, transmission rates, interference, and methods for keeping sensor and communication power loops separate. Two-way communications are frequently impossible (no service) or impractical, expensive, or power consumptive. Two-way methods (cellular, land line, radio, Internet) require smaller up-front costs as compared to other methods of communication and have variable recurrent costs, starting at zero. Satellite links work everywhere (except when blocked by trees or cliffs) and are quite reliable but are one-way and relatively slow, allow no re-transmissions, and require high up-front costs ($3000–4000) but no recurrent costs. Communications technology is changing constantly and requires vigilant attention by maintenance personnel.

1.4.6. Quality Assurance and Quality Control

Quality control and quality assurance are issues at every step through the entire sequence of sensing, communication, storage, retrieval, and display of environmental data. Quality assurance is an umbrella concept that covers all data collection and processing (start-to-finish) and ensures that credible information is available to the end user. Quality control has a more limited scope and is defined by the International Standards Organization as "the operational techniques and activities that are used to satisfy quality requirements." The central problem can be better appreciated if we approach quality control in the following way.

- Quality control is the evaluation, assessment, and rehabilitation of imperfect data by utilizing other imperfect data.

The quality of the data only decreases with time once the observation is made. The best and most effective quality control, therefore, consists in making high-quality measurements from the start and then successfully transmitting the measurements to an ingest process and storage site. Once the data are received from a monitoring station, a series of checks with increasing complexity can be applied, ranging from single-element checks (self-consistency) to multiple-element checks (inter-sensor consistency) to multiple-station/single-element checks (inter-station consistency). Suitable ancillary data (battery voltages, data ranges for all measurements, etc.) can prove extremely useful in diagnosing problems.

There is rarely a single technique in quality control procedures that will work satisfactorily for all situations. Quality-control procedures must be tailored to individual station circumstances, data access and storage methods, and climate regimes.

The fundamental issue in quality control centers on the tradeoff between falsely rejecting good data (Type I error) and falsely accepting bad data (Type II error). We cannot reduce the incidence of one type of error without increasing the incidence of the other type. In weather and climate data assessments, since good data are absolutely crucial for interpreting climate records properly, Type I errors are deemed far less desirable than Type II errors.

Not all observations are equal in importance. Quality-control procedures are likely to have the greatest difficulty evaluating the most extreme observations, where independent information usually must be sought and incorporated. Quality-control procedures involving more than one station usually involve a great deal of infrastructure with its own (imperfect) error-detection methods, which must be in place before a single value can be evaluated.

1.4.7. Standards
Although there is near-universal recognition of the value in systematic weather and climate measurements, these measurements will have little value unless they conform to accepted standards. There is not a single source for standards for collecting weather and climate data nor a single standard that meets all needs. Measurement standards have been developed by the World Meteorological Organization (WMO 1983; 2005), the American Association of State Climatologists (AASC 1985), the U.S. Environmental Protection Agency (EPA 1987), Finklin and Fischer (1990), the RAWS program (Bureau of Land Management [BLM] 1997), and the National Wildfire Coordinating Group (2004). Variations to these measurement standards also have been offered by instrument makers (e.g., Tanner 1990).

1.4.8. Who Makes the Measurements?
The lands under NPS stewardship provide many excellent locations to host the monitoring of climate by the NPS or other collaborators. These lands are largely protected from human development and other land changes that can impact observed climate records. Most park units historically have observed weather and climate elements as part of their overall mission. Many of these measurements come from station networks managed by other agencies, with observations taken or overseen by NPS personnel, in some cases, or by collaborators from the other agencies. National Park Service units that are small, lack sufficient resources, or lack sites presenting adequate exposure may benefit by utilizing weather and climate measurements collected from nearby stations.

2.0. Climate Background

The weather/climate vital sign is ranked first among all of the potential vital signs evaluated by the SFAN. Knowledge about weather and climate is critical because they affect not just geophysical and biological resources but ecosystem drivers and processes. Key reasons for monitoring weather and climate in network parks are because the effects can be long-lasting on (1) plant and animal populations, some of which are listed as endangered or threatened species, (2) on air and water quality, and (3) on drought and flood cycles, fires, mass wasting and other catastrophic events. Long-term weather data can also contribute to the understanding of global climate change and its effects on SFAN ecosystems (NPS 2005). It is essential that the SFAN park units have an effective climate monitoring system to track climate changes and to aid in management decisions relating to these changes. In order to do this, it is essential to understand the climate characteristics of the SFAN, as discussed in this chapter.

2.1. Climate and the SFAN Environment

Topography and coastal influences are instrumental in defining the climate of the SFAN (NPS 2005). Climate is associated with the broad-scale, long-term patterns of weather which drive the distribution and abundance of biota in a given region or biome. For the SFAN, topography and coastal influences are instrumental in defining the climate of the SFAN (NPS 2005). The temperature and precipitation patterns governing the flora and fauna in the SFAN are characterized by a moderate Mediterranean climate, with hot, dry summers and rainy, mild winters (NPS 2005). Snowfall is rare for SFAN park units. The most snowfall occurs at PINN, where one snow event usually occurs each year. Frost and short periods of freezing weather occur occasionally in winter and mostly in inland valleys, where park units like PINN can have freezing temperatures anytime between mid-November and mid-April. Coastal areas have a more moderate climate than the interior and can receive significant moisture from fog in summer. Inland areas receive about half the rainfall of areas along the coastal range. The SFAN climate offers long growing seasons (120-270 days; NWS 2003) and supports diverse plant and animal communities (Bailey 1995).

Changes in the frequency and duration of weather events such as those due to variations in the Pacific-North America Oscillation (PNA) cause changes in the onset and duration of the growing season, phenology and other aspects of natural disturbance regimes, and may alter natural communities and facilitate general change in species/habitat distributions (Spellerberg 1991; NPS 2005). Interannual climate variations due to the El Niño Southern Oscillation (ENSO) and the Pacific Decadal Oscillation (PDO) (Beamish and Bouillon 1993; Mantua 2000; Mantua and Hare 2002) also affect temperature and precipitation patterns and produce significant changes in abiotic and biotic ecosystem components (Thurman 1988). These changes are within the natural range of variation.

However, human activities may be altering the frequency and intensity of these events (NAST 2001). Climate changes due to human activities are expected to increase weather variability in unpredictable ways across the SFAN. The SFAN is predicted to have warmer temperatures, increased rainfall, and more intense and more frequent ENSO events (Bakun 1990; NAST 2001; NPS 2005). Models predict that sea levels will potentially rise from 5 to 37 inches over the next 100 years (NAST 2001).These changes will impact shoreline erosion rates, increase saltwater intrusion into groundwater supplies, and alter the water regimes of wetlands and estuaries. These are vital resource management concerns along the coastal SFAN park units. Increased and more intense precipitation would also increase erosion and flood events at all of the parks, where erodible soils are quite common (NPS 2005). Sea temperatures are also predicted to continue to rise. Central California waters have apparently increased in temperature over the past 30 years, with changes in the distribution of many marine species of invertebrates and fishes (Croll et al. 2000). Other potential consequences of future climate changes include changes in the initiation and duration of the growing season, increased drought occurrences, increased biological invasions, and shifting species ranges (NAST 2001; NPS 2005). Potential impacts to sensitive ecosystems, endemic species, and threatened or endangered species are of particular concern. A long-term meteorological monitoring program is essential to evaluate how meteorological change influences the functioning of ecosystems.

2.2. Spatial Variability

Mean annual precipitation for the SFAN is greatest along the coast (Figure 2.1). The highest precipitation totals are generally observed in portions of GOGA, MUWO, and PORE, where over 1000 mm of precipitation can occur each year. In contrast, PINN is further inland, in southeastern SFAN, and generally receives less than 500 mm of precipitation each year. As previously discussed, the SFAN exhibits a Mediterranean-type climate. As a result, precipitation falls primarily during the winter months (Figure 2.2).

Mean annual temperatures across the SFAN also exhibit a coast-interior gradient (Figure 2.3). The coolest park unit in the SFAN is PORE; mean annual temperatures in northwestern portions of the park unit do not exceed 12°C. The warmest conditions are found for JOMU and eastern portions of PINN, which both have mean annual temperatures near 14°C.

The coast-interior climate gradients in temperature are also well-defined during the winter and summer months. During the winter months, the coastal areas are the warmest. Many of the SFAN park units along the coast see January minimum temperatures above 4°C (Figure 2.4) and the park units nearer to downtown San Francisco (e.g., GOGA, PRSF) see January minimum temperatures that are closer to 6°C. On the other hand, January minimum temperatures at PINN are around -1°C or lower. The situation reverses in the summer months, with cooler conditions along the coast. For instance, July maximum temperatures are coolest in GOGA and FOPO, both of which are located along the coast. These park units struggle to get above 17°C during the month of July (Figure 2.5). In contrast, the warmest park unit is PINN, where July maximum temperatures can regularly exceed 35°C (also see NWS 2003).

The variability in SFAN climate produces many local microclimates. For example at PORE, Point Reyes Headland in the summer can struggle to get above 10°C with fog and wind, in contrast to Olema Valley, just 25 km distant, which sees temperatures approaching 30°C with much less wind (NWS 2003).

2.3. Temporal Variability

The PNA (Wallace and Gutzler 1981; Barnston and Livezey 1987) is an important contributor to variability of storm frequencies and tracks during a given year, with variations on the order of

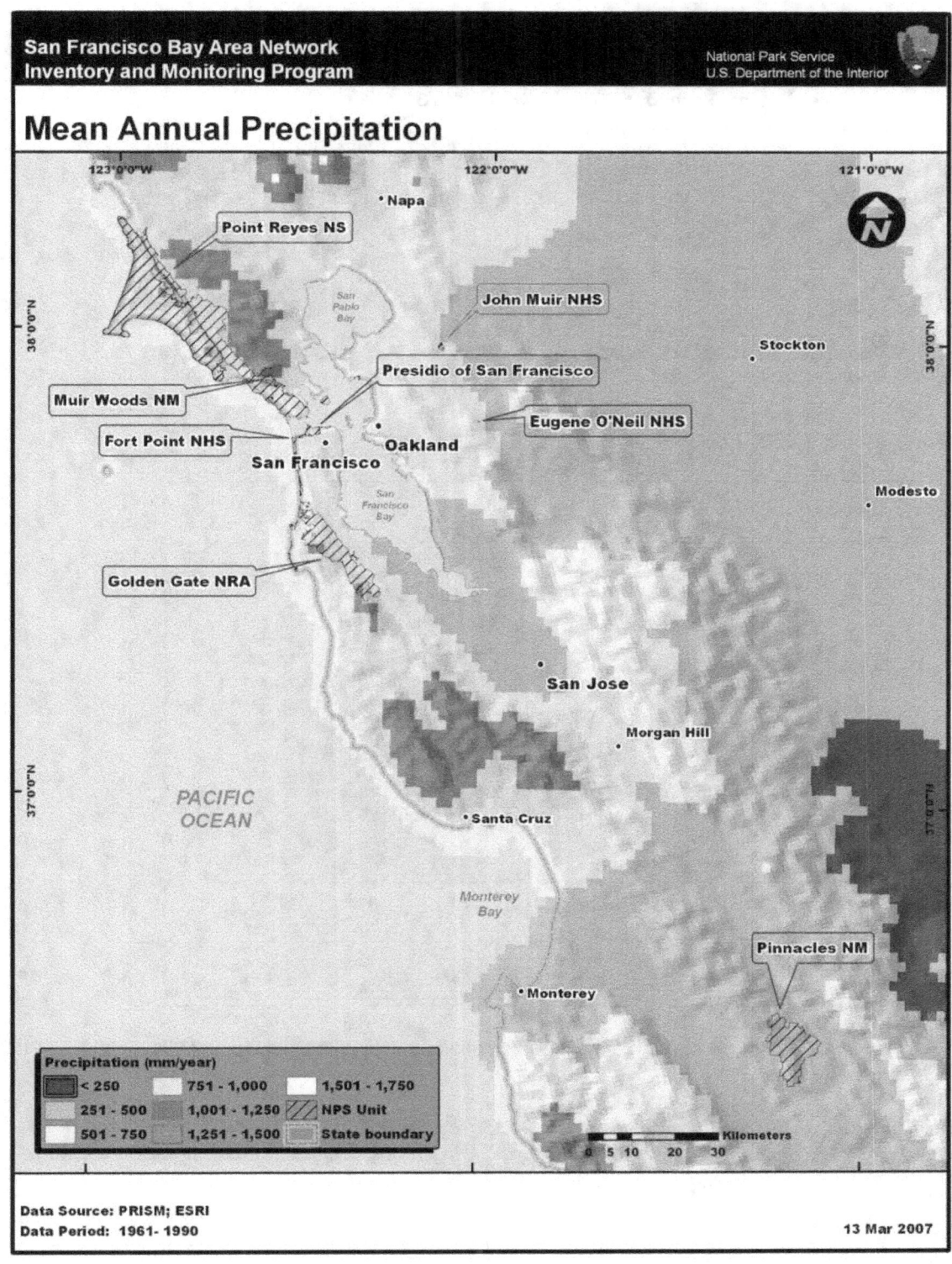

Figure 2.1. Mean annual precipitation, 1961-1990, for the SFAN.

a)

b)

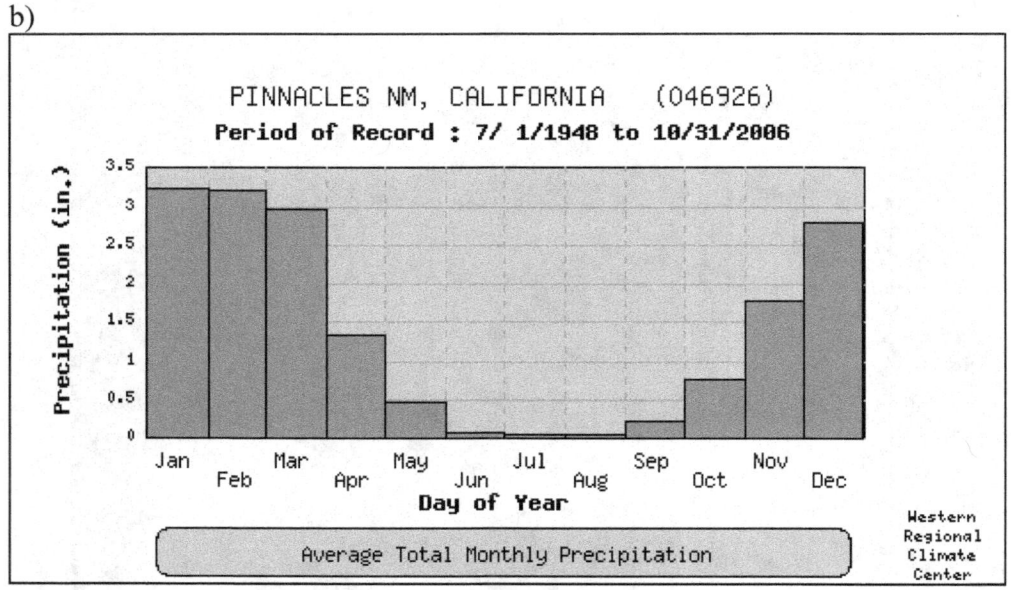

Figure 2.2. Mean monthly precipitation at selected locations in the SFAN, including MUWO (a) and PINN (b).

Mean Annual Temperature

Point Reyes NS

Napa

John Muir NHS

Presidio of San Francisco

Muir Woods NM

Eugene O'Neil NHS

Fort Point NHS

Oakland

San Francisco

Stockton

Modesto

Golden Gate NRA

San Jose

Morgan Hill

PACIFIC
OCEAN

Santa Cruz

Monterey
Bay

Pinnacles NM

Monterey

Temperature (deg C)

10	13.1 - 14	NPS Unit
10.1 - 11	14.1 - 15	State boundary
11.1 - 12	15.1 - 16	
12.1 - 13	16.1 - 17	

Kilometers
0 5 10   20   30

Data Source: PRISM; ESRI
Data Period: 1961- 1990

13 Mar 2007

Figure 2.3. Mean annual temperature, 1961-1990, for the SFAN.

Figure 2.4. Mean January minimum temperature, 1961-1990, for the SFAN.

Figure 2.5. Mean July maximum temperature, 1961-1990, for the SFAN.

weeks. Negative phases of the PNA generally bring cooler temperatures and increased storminess over the SFAN.

Both ENSO and PDO cause interannual climate variations in the SFAN (Redmond and Koch 1991; Mock 1996; Cayan et al. 1998; Mantua 2000; Mantua and Hare 2002). El Niño conditions and/or positive phases of the PDO are associated with wetter-than-normal conditions while La Niña conditions and/or negative phases of the PDO are associated with drier-than-normal conditions.

An investigation of daily precipitation amounts around the SFAN region over the last century (Figure 2.6) reveals little in the way of an overall trend, although precipitation appears to have increased over the SFAN since the 1930s. Long-term trends in ambient temperature (Figure 2.7) indicate that after a cool spell centered in the 1940s and 1950s, temperatures have become steadily warmer over the past 50 years. This finding is in line with other studies of temperature trends over the western U.S. (NAST 2001). However, it is not clear how much of this observed pattern may be due to discontinuities in temperature records at individual stations, caused by artificial changes such as station moves. These patterns highlight the emphasis on measurement consistency that is needed in order to properly detect long-term climatic changes.

2.4. Parameter Regression on Independent Slopes Model (PRISM)

The climate maps presented in this report were generated using the Parameter Regression on Independent Slopes Model (PRISM). This model was developed to address the extreme spatial and elevation gradients exhibited by the climate of the western U.S. (Daly et al. 1994; 2002; Gibson et al. 2002; Doggett et al. 2004). The maps produced through PRISM have undergone rigorous evaluation in the western U.S. This model was originally developed to provide climate information at scales matching available land-cover maps to assist in ecologic modeling. The PRISM technique accounts for the scale-dependent effects of topography on mean values of climate elements. Elevation provides the first-order constraint for the mapped climate fields, with slope and orientation (aspect) providing second-order constraints. The model has been enhanced gradually to address inversions, coast/land gradients, and climate patterns in small-scale trapping basins. Monthly climate fields are generated by PRISM to account for seasonal variations in elevation gradients in climate elements. These monthly climate fields then can be combined into seasonal and annual climate fields. Since PRISM maps are grid maps, they do not replicate point values but rather, for a given grid cell, represent the grid-cell average of the climate variable in question at the average elevation for that cell. The model relies on observed surface and upper-air measurements to estimate spatial climate fields.

Figure 2.6. Precipitation time series, 1895-2005, for the SFAN region. These include twelve-month precipitation (ending in December) (red), 10-year running mean (blue), mean (green), and plus/minus one standard deviation (green dotted).

Figure 2.7. Temperature time series, 1895-2005, for the SFAN region. These include twelve-month average temperature (ending in December) (red), 10-year running mean (blue), mean (green), and plus/minus one standard deviation (green dotted).

3.0. Methods

Having discussed the climatic characteristics of the SFAN, we now present the procedures that were used to obtain information for weather and climate stations within the SFAN. This information was obtained from various sources, as mentioned in the following paragraphs. Retrieval of station metadata constituted a major component of this work.

3.1. Metadata Retrieval

A key component of station inventories is determining the kinds of observations that have been conducted over time, by whom, and in what manner; when each type of observation began and ended; and whether these observations are still being conducted. Metadata about the observational process (Table 3.1) generally consist of a series of vignettes that apply to time intervals and, therefore, constitute a *history* rather than a single snapshot. An expanded list of relevant metadata fields for this inventory is provided in Appendix E. This report has relied on metadata records from three sources: (a) Western Regional Climate Center (WRCC), (b) NPS personnel, and (c) other knowledgeable personnel, such as state climate office staff.

The initial metadata sources for this report were stored at WRCC. This regional climate center (RCC) acts as a working repository of many western climate records, including the main networks outlined in this section. The WRCC conducts live and periodic data collection (ingests) from all major national and western weather and climate networks. These networks include the COOP network, the Surface Airways Observation network (SAO) operated by NWS and the Federal Aviation Administration (FAA), the interagency RAWS network, and various smaller networks. The WRCC is expanding its capability to ingest information from other networks as resources permit and usefulness dictates. This center has relied heavily on historic archives (in many cases supplemented with live ingests) to assess the quantity (not necessarily quality) of data available for NPS I&M network applications.

The primary source of metadata at WRCC is the Applied Climate Information System (ACIS), a joint effort among RCCs and other NOAA entities. Metadata for SFAN weather and climate stations identified from the ACIS database are available in file "SFAN_from_ACIS.tar.gz" (see Appendix F). Historic metadata pertaining to major climate- and weather-observing systems in the U.S. are stored in ACIS where metadata are linked to the observed data. A distributed system, ACIS is synchronized among the RCCs. Mainstream software is utilized, including Postgress, Python™, and Java™ programming languages; CORBA®-compliant network software; and industry-standard, nonproprietary hardware and software. Metadata and data for all major national climate and weather networks have been entered into the ACIS database. For this project, the available metadata from many smaller networks also have been entered but in most cases the actual data have not yet been entered. Data sets are in the NetCDF (Network Common Data Form) format, but the design allows for integration with legacy systems, including non-NetCDF files (used at WRCC) and additional metadata (added for this project). The ACIS also supports a suite of products to visualize or summarize data from these data sets. National climate-monitoring maps are updated daily using the ACIS data feed. The developmental phases of ACIS have utilized metadata supplied by the NCDC and NWS with many tens of thousands of entries, screened as well as possible for duplications, mistakes, and omissions.

Table 3.1. Primary metadata fields for SFAN weather and climate stations. Explanations are provided as appropriate.

Metadata Field	Notes
Station name	Station name associated with network listed in "Climate Network."
Latitude	Numerical value (units: see coordinate units).
Longitude	Numerical value (units: see coordinate units).
Coordinate units	Latitude/longitude (units: decimal degrees, degree-minute-second, etc.).
Datum	Datum used as basis for coordinates: WGS 84, NAD 83, etc.
Elevation	Elevation of station above mean sea level (m).
Slope	Slope of ground surface below station (degrees).
Aspect	Azimuth that ground surface below station faces.
Climate division	NOAA climate division where station is located. Climate divisions are NOAA-specified zones sharing similar climate and hydrology characteristics.
Country	Country where station is located.
State	State where station is located.
County	County where station is located.
Weather/climate network	Primary weather/climate network the station belongs to (COOP, RAWS, etc.).
NPS unit code	Four-letter code identifying park unit where station resides.
NPS unit name	Full name of park unit.
NPS unit type	National park, national monument, etc.
UTM zone	If UTM is the only coordinate system available.
Location notes	Useful information not already included in "station narrative."
Climate variables	Temperature, precipitation, etc.
Installation date	Date of station installation.
Removal date	Date of station removal.
Station photograph	Digital image of station.
Photograph date	Date photograph was taken.
Photographer	Name of person who took the photograph.
Station narrative	Anything related to general site description; may include site exposure, characteristics of surrounding vegetation, driving directions, etc.
Contact name	Name of the person involved with station operation.
Organization	Group or agency affiliation of contact person.
Contact type	Designation that identifies contact person as the station owner, observer, maintenance person, data manager, etc.
Position/job title	Official position/job title of contact person.
Address	Address of contact person.
E-mail address	E-mail address of contact person.
Phone	Phone number of contact person (and extension if available).
Contact notes	Other information needed to reach contact person.

Two types of information have been used to complete the SFAN climate station inventory.

- Station inventories: Information about observational procedures, latitude/longitude, elevation, measured elements, measurement frequency, sensor types, exposures, ground cover and vegetation, data-processing details, network, purpose, and managing individual or agency, etc.

- Data inventories: Information about measured data values including completeness, seasonality, data gaps, representation of missing data, flagging systems, how special circumstances in the data record are denoted, etc.

This is not a straightforward process. Extensive searches are typically required to develop historic station and data inventories. Both types of inventories frequently contain information gaps and often rely on tacit and unrealistic assumptions. Sources of information for these inventories frequently are difficult to recover or are undocumented and unreliable. In many cases, the actual weather/climate data available from different sources are not linked directly to metadata records. To the extent that actual data can be acquired (rather than just metadata), it is possible to cross-check these records and perform additional assessments based on the amount and completeness of the data.

Certain types of weather and climate networks that possess any of the following attributes have not been considered for inclusion in the inventory:

- Private networks with proprietary access and/or inability to obtain or provide sufficient metadata.
- Private weather enthusiasts (often with high-quality data) whose metadata are not available and whose data are not readily accessible.
- Unofficial observers supplying data to the NWS (lack of access to current data and historic archives; lack of metadata).
- Networks having no available historic data.
- Networks having poor-quality metadata.
- Networks having poor access to metadata.
- Real-time networks having poor access to real-time data.

Previous inventory efforts at WRCC have shown that for the networks identified in the preceding list, in light of the need for quality data to track weather and climate, the resources required and difficulty encountered in obtaining metadata or data are prohibitively large.

3.2. Criteria for Locating Stations

To identify weather and climate stations for each park unit in the SFAN we selected only those stations located within a specified buffer distance of the SFAN park units. These buffer distances were 40 km for both PINN and PORE, and 20 km for the other SFAN park units. These distances were selected in an attempt to include automated stations from major networks such as RAWS and SAO for park units such as PINN and PORE, but also to keep the size of the stations lists to a reasonable number for the SFAN park units in the San Francisco metropolitan area.

The station locator maps presented in Chapter 4 were designed to show clearly the spatial distributions of all major weather and climate station networks in SFAN. We recognize that other mapping formats may be more suitable for other specific needs.

4.0. Station Inventory

An objective of this report is to show the locations of weather and climate stations for the SFAN region in relation to the boundaries of the NPS park units within the SFAN. A station does not have to be within park boundaries to provide useful data and information for a park unit.

4.1. Climate and Weather Networks

Most stations in the SFAN region are associated with at least one of 13 major weather and climate networks (Table 4.1). Brief descriptions of each weather/climate network are provided below (see Appendix G for greater detail).

Table 4.1. Weather and climate networks represented within the SFAN.

Acronym	Name
BAMI	Bay Area Mesoscale Initiative network
CARB	California Air Resources Board network
CASTNet	Clean Air Status and Trends Network
CIMIS	California Irrigation Management Information System
COOP	NWS Cooperative Observer Program
CWOP	Citizen Weather Observer Program
DRI	Desert Research Institute network
GPMP	NPS Gaseous Pollutant Monitoring Program
GPS-MET	NOAA ground-based GPS meteorology network
NADP	National Atmospheric Deposition Program
RAWS	Remote Automated Weather Station network
SAO	NWS/FAA Surface Airways Observation network
WX4U	Weather For You network

4.1.1. Bay Area Mesoscale Initiative (BAMI) Network

The BAMI network is a series of automated weather stations that are installed around the Bay Area with the purpose of monitoring local weather phenomena such as fog dynamics. Unfortunately, many of these stations are not currently active.

4.1.2. California Air Resources Board (CARB) Network

Meteorological measurements are taken at CARB sites in support of their overall mission of promoting and protecting public health, welfare and ecological resources in California through the reduction of air pollutants, while accounting for economical effects of such measures. Measured elements include temperature, relative humidity, precipitation, and wind speed and direction.

4.1.3. Clean Air Status and Trends Network (CASTNet)

CASTNet is primarily an air-quality monitoring network managed by the EPA. Standard hourly weather and climate elements are measured and include temperature, wind, humidity, solar radiation, soil temperature, and sometimes moisture. These elements are intended to support interpretation of air-quality parameters that also are measured at CASTNet sites. Data records at CASTNet sites are generally one–two decades in length.

4.1.4. California Irrigation Management Information System (CIMIS)

The CIMIS network, operated through the California Department of Water Resources, is a network of over 120 automated weather stations in the state of California. CIMIS stations are used to assist irrigators in managing their water resources efficiently. Measured meteorological elements at CIMIS stations generally include temperature, precipitation, wind, and solar radiation. Some stations measure additional parameters such as soil temperature and moisture.

4.1.5. NWS Cooperative Observer Program (COOP)

The COOP network has been a foundation of the U.S. climate program for decades and continues to play an important role. Manual measurements are made by volunteers and consist of daily maximum and minimum temperatures, observation-time temperature, daily precipitation, daily snowfall, and snow depth. When blended with NWS measurements, the data set is known as SOD, or "Summary of the Day." The quality of data from COOP sites ranges from excellent to modest.

4.1.6. Citizen Weather Observer Program (CWOP)

The CWOP network consists primarily of automated weather stations operated by private citizens who have either an Internet connection and/or a wireless Ham radio setup. Data from CWOP stations are specifically intended for use in research, education, and homeland security activities. Although standard meteorological elements such as temperature, precipitation, and wind are measured at all CWOP stations, station characteristics do vary, including sensor types and site exposure.

4.1.7. Desert Research Institute (DRI) Network

The Desert Research Institute (DRI) operates this network of automated weather stations, located primarily in California and Western Nevada. Many of these stations are located in remote mountain and desert locations and provide data that are often used in support of various mountain- and desert-based environmental studies in the region. Meteorology elements are measured every 10 minutes and include temperature, wind, humidity, barometric pressure, precipitation, and solar radiation.

4.1.8. Gaseous Pollutant Monitoring Program (GPMP)

The GPMP network measures hourly meteorological data in support of pollutant monitoring activities. Measured elements include temperature, precipitation, humidity, wind, solar radiation, and surface wetness. These data are generally of high quality, with records extending up to two decades in length.

4.1.9. NOAA Ground-Based GPS Meteorology (GPS-MET) Network

The GPS-MET network is the first network of its kind dedicated to Global Positioning System (GPS) meteorology (see Duan et al. 1996). GPS meteorology utilizes the radio signals broadcast by GPS satellites for atmospheric remote sensing. GPS meteorology applications have evolved along two paths: ground-based (Bevis et al. 1992) and space-based (Yuan et al. 1993). For more information, please see Appendix G. The stations identified in this inventory are all ground-based. The GPS-MET network was developed in response to the need for improved moisture observations to support weather forecasting, climate monitoring, and other research activities. The primary goals of this network are to measure atmospheric water vapor using ground-based GPS receivers, facilitate the operational use of these data, and encourage usage of GPS meteorology for atmospheric research and other applications. GPS-MET is a collaboration between NOAA and several other governmental and university organizations and institutions. Ancillary meteorological observations at GPS-MET stations include temperature, relative humidity, and barometric pressure.

4.1.10. National Atmospheric Deposition Program (NADP)

The purpose of the NADP network is to monitor primarily wet deposition at selected sites around the U.S. and its territories. The network is a collaborative effort among several agencies including USDA and the U.S. Geological Survey (USGS). Precipitation is the primary climate parameter measured at NADP sites. This network includes stations from the Mercury Deposition Network (MDN).

4.1.11. Remote Automated Weather Station (RAWS) Network

The RAWS network is administered through many land management agencies, particularly the BLM and the Forest Service. Hourly meteorology elements are measured and include temperature, wind, humidity, solar radiation, barometric pressure, fuel temperature, and precipitation (when temperatures are above freezing). The fire community is the primary client for RAWS data. These sites are remote and data typically are transmitted via GOES (Geostationary Operational Environmental Satellite). Some sites operate all winter. Most data records for RAWS sites began during or after the mid-1980s.

4.1.12. NWS Surface Airways Observation Network (SAO)

These stations are located usually at major airports and military bases. Almost all SAO sites are automated. The hourly data measured at these sites include temperature, precipitation, humidity, wind, barometric pressure, sky cover, ceiling, visibility, and current weather. Most data records begin during or after the 1940s, and these data are generally of high quality.

4.1.13. Weather For You Network (WX4U)

The WX4U network is a nationwide collection of weather stations run by local observers. Data quality varies with site. Standard meteorological elements are measured and usually include temperature, precipitation, wind, and relative humidity.

4.1.14. Weather Bureau Army Navy (WBAN)

Some stations are identified in this report as WBAN stations. This is a station identification system rather than a true weather/climate network. Stations identified with WBAN are largely historical stations that reported meteorological observations on the WBAN weather observation forms that were common during the early and middle parts of the twentieth century. The use of WBAN numbers to identify stations was one of the first attempts in the U.S. to use a coordinated station numbering scheme between several weather station networks, such as the COOP and SAO networks.

4.1.15. Other Networks

In addition to the major networks mentioned above, there are various networks that are operated for specific purposes by specific organizations or governmental agencies or scientific research projects. These networks could be present within SFAN but have not been identified in this report. Some of the commonly used networks include the following:

- NOAA upper-air stations
- Federal and state departments of transportation
- U.S. Department of Energy Surface Radiation Budget Network (Surfrad)
- Park-specific-monitoring networks and stations
- Other research or project networks having many possible owners

4.2. Station Locations

The major weather/climate networks in the SFAN (discussed in Section 4.1) have at most several stations at or inside each park unit (Table 4.2). The COOP network generally has the most stations within park units of any of the weather/climate networks we identified for SFAN.

Table 4.2. Number of stations within or nearby SFAN park units. Numbers are listed by park unit and by weather/climate network. Figures in parentheses indicate the numbers of stations within park boundaries.

Network	EUON	FOPO	GOGA	JOMU	MUWO	PINN	PORE	PRSF
BAMI	0(0)	1(0)	1(0)	0(0)	1(0)	0(0)	1(0)	1(0)
CARB	5(0)	6(0)	11(1)	7(0)	4(0)	3(1)	10(1)	7(0)
CASTNet	0(0)	0(0)	0(0)	0(0)	0(0)	1(1)	0(0)	0(0)
CIMIS	4(0)	1(0)	4(1)	3(0)	1(0)	8(0)	8(0)	1(0)
COOP	32(0)	17(0)	49(3)	33(0)	16(0)	24(1)	43(2)	18(2)
CWOP	18(0)	9(0)	30(1)	17(0)	7(0)	2(0)	29(0)	11(0)
DRI	0(0)	0(0)	2(0)	0(0)	0(0)	0(0)	2(2)	0(0)
GPMP	0(0)	0(0)	1(0)	0(0)	0(0)	1(1)	1(1)	0(0)
GPS-MET	0(0)	0(0)	1(0)	0(0)	0(0)	0(0)	1(0)	0(0)
NADP	0(0)	0(0)	0(0)	0(0)	0(0)	1(1)	0(0)	0(0)
RAWS	5(0)	2(0)	11(3)	3(0)	5(0)	6(1)	7(1)	2(0)
SAO	4(0)	6(0)	13(3)	3(0)	5(0)	1(0)	12(1)	6(1)
WX4U	4(0)	2(0)	10(1)	1(0)	2(0)	0(0)	7(0)	2(0)
Other	0(0)	4(0)	10(0)	2(0)	3(1)	2(0)	10(0)	4(0)
Total	72(0)	48(0)	143(13)	69(0)	44(1)	49(6)	131(8)	52(3)

Lists of stations have been compiled for the SFAN. As previously noted, a station does not have to be within park unit boundaries to provide useful data and information regarding a given park unit. Some might be physically *within* the administrative or political boundaries, whereas others might be just outside, or even some distance away, but would be *nearby* in terms of behavior and representativeness. What constitutes "useful" and "representative" are also significant questions, whose answers can vary according to application, type of element, period of record, procedural or methodological observation conventions, and the like.

4.2.1. North Bay Area

We identified 13 weather/climate stations within the boundaries of GOGA (Table 4.3; Figure 4.1; Figure 4.2). All but four of these stations are active currently. The CARB station "Fort Funston" is located west of Daly City. The CIMIS station "Woodside" is in the extreme southern

Table 4.3. Weather and climate stations for the SFAN park units in the north Bay Area. Stations inside park units and within a specified buffer distance (40 km for PORE; 20 km for other park units) of the park unit boundary are included. Missing entries are indicated by "M".

Name	Lat.	Lon.	Elev. (m)	Network	Start	End	In Park?
Golden Gate National Recreation Area (GOGA)							
Fort Funston	37.713	-122.499	17	CARB	M	Present	Yes
Woodside	37.453	-122.280	171	CIMIS	M	Present	Yes
Crissy Field	37.800	-122.467	2	COOP	5/1/1928	6/30/1936	Yes
Fort Point	37.800	-122.467	3	COOP	3/1/1951	3/2/2000	Yes
Mount Tamalpais 2 SW	37.903	-122.603	447	COOP	2/1/1898	Present	Yes
KE6FWD Mill Valley	37.908	-122.576	294	CWOP	M	Present	Yes
Golden Gate NRA #1	37.833	-122.535	457	RAWS	7/1/1995	11/30/1999	Yes
Pulgas	37.475	-122.298	196	RAWS	5/1/1997	Present	Yes
Spring Valley	37.563	-122.436	328	RAWS	10/1/1998	Present	Yes
Crissy	37.800	-122.467	6	SAO	12/1/1922	4/30/1936	Yes
Point Bonita Sausalito	37.817	-122.533	1	SAO	9/1/1972	Present	Yes
Point Blunt Sausalito	37.850	-122.417	73	SAO	10/1/1972	Present	Yes
Burlingame	37.480	-122.330	46	WX4U	M	Present	Yes
BAMI6	37.950	-122.400	111	BAMI	M	Present	No
Mount Tamalpais	37.926	-122.587	232	CARB	M	Present	No
Point Reyes National Seashore	38.123	-122.908	100	CARB	M	Present	No
Richmond-7th Street	37.948	-122.365	11	CARB	M	Present	No
San Carlos	37.517	-122.252	0	CARB	M	Present	No
San Fran Sewage Treat. Plt.	37.739	-122.390	2	CARB	M	Present	No
San Francisco-Hunters Point	37.734	-122.383	250	CARB	M	Present	No
San Pablo - El Portal	37.963	-122.340	15	CARB	M	Present	No
San Pablo-Rumrill Blvd.	37.960	-122.356	9	CARB	M	Present	No
Stanford University	37.430	-122.187	36	CARB	M	Present	No
Valley Ford	38.307	-122.896	5	CARB	M	Present	No
Black Point	38.091	-122.527	0	CIMIS	6/1/2003	Present	No
Novato	38.121	-122.543	8	CIMIS	7/1/1986	1/31/2002	No
Point San Pedro	37.992	-122.470	2	CIMIS	12/1/2002	Present	No
Alvarado	37.600	-122.117	3	COOP	1/1/1931	4/30/1942	No
Berkeley	37.874	-122.259	94	COOP	1/1/1893	Present	No
Black Mtn 2 WSW	37.317	-122.167	646	COOP	1/1/1943	7/1/1995	No
Burlingame	37.583	-122.350	3	COOP	12/8/1906	6/30/1978	No
El Granada	37.500	-122.450	49	COOP	2/1/1953	4/30/1953	No
Half Moon Bay	37.473	-122.443	8	COOP	7/1/1939	Present	No
Hamilton AFB	38.067	-122.517	4	COOP	2/1/1934	1/31/1976	No
Hamilton AFB 1 E	38.050	-122.500	3	COOP	5/1/1955	8/31/1959	No
Kentfield	37.957	-122.544	44	COOP	1/1/1902	Present	No
La Honda	37.317	-122.267	229	COOP	1/1/1950	9/30/1977	No
Mount Tamalpais	37.917	-122.583	793	COOP	12/1/1956	Present	No
Muir Woods	37.898	-122.569	67	COOP	12/1/1940	Present	No
Novato 8 WNW	38.133	-122.717	122	COOP	7/1/1948	10/23/1996	No
Oakland	37.721	-122.221	2	COOP	5/1/1928	Present	No

Name	Lat.	Lon.	Elev. (m)	Network	Start	End	In Park?
Oakland City Hall	37.800	-122.267	11	COOP	5/1/1949	11/30/1954	No
Oakland Light Stn.	37.800	-122.317	0	COOP	M	Present	No
Oakland Museum	37.798	-122.264	9	COOP	10/1/1970	Present	No
Occidental	38.386	-122.966	264	COOP	5/1/1940	Present	No
Orinda	37.883	-122.200	113	COOP	5/1/1953	Present	No
Pacifica	37.611	-122.484	38	COOP	9/22/2000	Present	No
Pacifica 4 SSE	37.592	-122.472	145	COOP	7/1/1983	Present	No
Palo Alto	37.433	-122.167	18	COOP	3/1/1906	8/31/1953	No
Palo Alto	37.444	-122.139	8	COOP	9/1/1953	Present	No
Pescadero 3 E	37.261	-122.328	28	COOP	6/1/1994	9/13/2005	No
Point Montara Light	37.533	-122.517	27	COOP	4/1/1943	3/31/1956	No
Point Reyes Alert	38.101	-122.930	53	COOP	2/2/1993	Present	No
Point Reyes Light Stn.	38.000	-123.017	88	COOP	1/1/1899	Present	No
Point Reyes Stn.	38.067	-122.800	9	COOP	1/1/1931	4/30/1936	No
Redwood City	37.477	-122.239	9	COOP	4/1/1906	Present	No
Redwood City	37.488	-122.214	3	COOP	1/1/1997	Present	No
Richmond	37.919	-122.377	6	COOP	12/1/1950	Present	No
Richmond Field Stn.	37.917	-122.333	3	COOP	8/1/1955	9/30/1959	No
Round Top	37.850	-122.200	537	COOP	7/1/1943	Present	No
San Francisco	37.769	-122.433	53	COOP	10/1/1849	Present	No
San Francisco Acad. O.	37.767	-122.467	76	COOP	7/1/1951	8/31/1957	No
San Francisco Intl. Arpt.	37.658	-122.438	2	COOP	5/1/1928	Present	No
San Francisco Oceans	37.728	-122.504	2	COOP	7/1/1948	Present	No
San Gregorio	37.304	-122.361	84	COOP	5/1/1954	Present	No
San Mateo	37.533	-122.300	6	COOP	3/1/1906	12/31/1978	No
San Rafael Civic Center	37.998	-122.537	37	COOP	1/1/1894	Present	No
Sausalito	37.850	-122.483	0	COOP	1/1/1904	6/30/1914	No
Searsville Lake	37.400	-122.233	107	COOP	9/1/1925	1/1/1973	No
Sky Londa	37.350	-122.267	451	COOP	4/1/1953	Present	No
Skyline Ridge	37.313	-122.184	692	COOP	7/1/1995	Present	No
Woodacre	37.983	-122.583	128	COOP	4/1/1953	Present	No
Woodside Fire Stn 1	37.429	-122.257	116	COOP	1/1/1973	Present	No
AD6WX Mill Valley	37.886	-122.532	107	CWOP	M	Present	No
CW0013 Inverness	38.073	-122.844	290	CWOP	M	Present	No
CW0277 Alameda	37.759	-122.238	2	CWOP	M	Present	No
CW0553 Belmont	37.514	-122.295	91	CWOP	M	Present	No
CW0791 Belmont	37.503	-122.307	233	CWOP	M	Present	No
CW0879 Hercules	38.007	-122.277	42	CWOP	M	Present	No
CW0888 Pacifica	37.647	-122.474	207	CWOP	M	Present	No
CW0963 Daly City	37.667	-122.488	153	CWOP	M	Present	No
CW1194 San Mateo	37.563	-122.324	50	CWOP	M	Present	No
CW1362 Hayward	37.602	-122.123	10	CWOP	M	Present	No
CW1634 Berkeley	37.856	-122.244	110	CWOP	M	Present	No
CW1751 San Francisco	37.780	-122.476	30	CWOP	M	Present	No
CW2054 Pacifica	37.638	-122.494	25	CWOP	M	Present	No
CW3073 Woodside	37.384	-122.247	311	CWOP	M	Present	No

Name	Lat.	Lon.	Elev. (m)	Network	Start	End	In Park?
CW3295 Half Moon Bay	37.511	-122.487	18	CWOP	M	Present	No
CW3537 Novato	38.084	-122.568	15	CWOP	M	Present	No
CW3602 San Rafael	37.997	-122.467	20	CWOP	M	Present	No
CW3879 El Sobrante	37.976	-122.305	99	CWOP	M	Present	No
CW4751 Belmont	37.517	-122.309	109	CWOP	M	Present	No
CW4832 Los Altos Hills	37.384	-122.146	112	CWOP	M	Present	No
CW4846 Portola Valley	37.387	-122.211	201	CWOP	M	Present	No
CW5006 Foster City	37.564	-122.263	1	CWOP	M	Present	No
K6DJR W.Menlo Park	37.435	-122.206	35	CWOP	M	Present	No
KA6TGI Daly City	37.705	-122.430	177	CWOP	M	Present	No
KF6YUA Sebastopol	38.380	-122.824	70	CWOP	M	Present	No
KG6PPD Mountain View	37.376	-122.082	41	CWOP	M	Present	No
N6WKZ San Francisco	37.752	-122.453	200	CWOP	M	Present	No
WA6LCN Marinwood	38.030	-122.545	40	CWOP	M	Present	No
WW6HAM Pacifica	37.645	-122.472	195	CWOP	M	Present	No
Pt. Reyes Lighthouse	37.996	-123.021	160	DRI	10/1/2006	Present	No
Pt. Reyes RCA	38.094	-122.950	27	DRI	10/1/2006	Present	No
Point Reyes R.S.	38.123	-122.908	76	GPMP	11/1/1987	12/31/1992	No
Bodega Bay	38.320	-123.070	15	GPS-MET	M	Present	No
Barnaby	38.028	-122.702	378	RAWS	1/1/1997	Present	No
Big Rock	38.039	-122.570	457	RAWS	9/1/2003	Present	No
La Honda	37.305	-122.254	130	RAWS	5/1/1990	Present	No
Los Altos	37.358	-122.147	197	RAWS	2/1/1998	Present	No
Middle Peak	37.931	-122.591	759	RAWS	5/1/2004	Present	No
Oakland North	37.875	-122.217	152	RAWS	6/1/1992	Present	No
Olema Valley	38.043	-122.796	11	RAWS	5/1/2005	Present	No
Woodacre	37.991	-122.645	427	RAWS	5/1/2003	Present	No
Alameda	37.733	-122.317	5	SAO	7/1/1941	Present	No
Bodega Bay Station	38.317	-123.050	3	SAO	4/8/1971	Present	No
Hamilton AFB	38.067	-122.517	4	SAO	2/1/1934	1/31/1976	No
Oakland	37.721	-122.221	2	SAO	5/1/1928	Present	No
Palo Alto	37.467	-122.117	1	SAO	5/1/1928	Present	No
Pillar Point	37.500	-122.500	40	SAO	2/1/1973	Present	No
Point Reyes Light Stn.	38.000	-123.017	88	SAO	1/1/1899	Present	No
San Carlos	37.517	-122.250	1	SAO	9/1/1969	Present	No
San Francisco Intl. Arpt.	37.658	-122.438	2	SAO	5/1/1928	Present	No
San Francisco PBS	37.750	-122.683	5	SAO	11/1/1973	Present	No
Mount Tamalpais	37.900	-122.583	290	WBAN	7/1/1940	10/31/1957	No
Mount Tamalpais	37.933	-122.583	724	WBAN	11/1/1898	2/28/1955	No
Oakland	37.800	-122.350	5	WBAN	1/1/1943	6/30/1943	No
Point Au Nuevo	37.350	-122.367	141	WBAN	6/1/1943	10/31/1944	No
Point Montara	37.533	-122.517	12	WBAN	3/1/1938	12/31/1962	No
San Francisco	37.783	-122.317	5	WBAN	10/1/1931	12/31/1933	No
San Pablo	37.983	-122.350	79	WBAN	5/1/1928	3/31/1939	No
San Rafael Hamilton	38.050	-122.500	1	WBAN	5/1/1935	5/31/1947	No
Sunnyvale	37.417	-122.050	8	WBAN	8/1/1932	10/31/1935	No

Name	Lat.	Lon.	Elev. (m)	Network	Start	End	In Park?
Vallejo	38.000	-122.333	14	WBAN	7/1/1942	8/31/1943	No
Belmont	37.520	-122.290	30	WX4U	M	Present	No
Corte Madera	37.930	-122.520	3	WX4U	M	Present	No
Dimond District Oakland	37.796	-122.208	52	WX4U	M	Present	No
Emerald Hills Redwood City	37.460	-122.270	80	WX4U	M	Present	No
Half Moon Bay	37.460	-122.440	12	WX4U	M	Present	No
Oakland	37.800	-122.210	122	WX4U	M	Present	No
Occidental	38.370	-123.000	223	WX4U	M	Present	No
Pickles Central San Rafael	37.980	-122.520	54	WX4U	M	Present	No
Sebastopol	38.370	-122.820	61	WX4U	M	Present	No
Muir Woods National Monument (MUWO)							
Mount Tamalpais	37.900	-122.583	290	WBAN	7/1/1940	10/31/1957	Yes
BAMI6	37.950	-122.400	111	BAMI	M	Present	No
Fort Funston	37.713	-122.499	17	CARB	M	Present	No
Mount Tamalpais	37.926	-122.587	232	CARB	M	Present	No
Richmond-7th Street	37.948	-122.365	11	CARB	M	Present	No
San Pablo-Rumrill Blvd.	37.960	-122.356	9	CARB	M	Present	No
Point San Pedro	37.992	-122.470	2	CIMIS	12/1/2002	Present	No
Crissy Field	37.800	-122.467	2	COOP	5/1/1928	6/30/1936	No
Fort Point	37.800	-122.467	3	COOP	3/1/1951	3/2/2000	No
Hamilton AFB	38.067	-122.517	4	COOP	2/1/1934	1/31/1976	No
Hamilton AFB 1 E	38.050	-122.500	3	COOP	5/1/1955	8/31/1959	No
Kentfield	37.957	-122.544	44	COOP	1/1/1902	Present	No
Mount Tamalpais	37.917	-122.583	793	COOP	12/1/1956	Present	No
Mount Tamalpais 2 SW	37.903	-122.603	447	COOP	2/1/1898	Present	No
Muir Woods	37.898	-122.569	67	COOP	12/1/1940	Present	No
Richmond	37.919	-122.377	6	COOP	12/1/1950	Present	No
Richmond Field Stn.	37.917	-122.333	3	COOP	8/1/1955	9/30/1959	No
San Francisco	37.769	-122.433	53	COOP	10/1/1849	Present	No
San Francisco Acad. O.	37.767	-122.467	76	COOP	7/1/1951	8/31/1957	No
San Francisco Oceans	37.728	-122.504	2	COOP	7/1/1948	Present	No
San Rafael Civic Center	37.998	-122.537	37	COOP	1/1/1894	Present	No
Sausalito	37.850	-122.483	0	COOP	1/1/1904	6/30/1914	No
Woodacre	37.983	-122.583	128	COOP	4/1/1953	Present	No
AD6WX Mill Valley	37.886	-122.532	107	CWOP	M	Present	No
CW1751 San Francisco	37.780	-122.476	30	CWOP	M	Present	No
CW3537 Novato	38.084	-122.568	15	CWOP	M	Present	No
CW3602 San Rafael	37.997	-122.467	20	CWOP	M	Present	No
KE6FWD Mill Valley	37.908	-122.576	294	CWOP	M	Present	No
N6WKZ San Francisco	37.752	-122.453	200	CWOP	M	Present	No
WA6LCN Marinwood	38.030	-122.545	40	CWOP	M	Present	No
Barnaby	38.028	-122.702	378	RAWS	1/1/1997	Present	No
Big Rock	38.039	-122.570	457	RAWS	9/1/2003	Present	No
Golden Gate NRA #1	37.833	-122.535	457	RAWS	7/1/1995	11/30/1999	No
Middle Peak	37.931	-122.591	759	RAWS	5/1/2004	Present	No

Name	Lat.	Lon.	Elev. (m)	Network	Start	End	In Park?
Woodacre	37.991	-122.645	427	RAWS	5/1/2003	Present	No
Crissy	37.800	-122.467	6	SAO	12/1/1922	4/30/1936	No
Hamilton AFB	38.067	-122.517	4	SAO	2/1/1934	1/31/1976	No
Point Blunt Sausalito	37.850	-122.417	73	SAO	10/1/1972	Present	No
Point Bonita Sausalito	37.817	-122.533	1	SAO	9/1/1972	Present	No
San Francisco PBS	37.750	-122.683	5	SAO	11/1/1973	Present	No
Mount Tamalpais	37.933	-122.583	724	WBAN	11/1/1898	2/28/1955	No
San Rafael Hamilton	38.050	-122.500	1	WBAN	5/1/1935	5/31/1947	No
Corte Madera	37.930	-122.520	3	WX4U	M	Present	No
Pickles Central San Rafael	37.980	-122.520	54	WX4U	M	Present	No
Point Reyes National Seashore (PORE)							
Point Reyes Natl. Seashore	38.123	-122.908	100	CARB	M	Present	Yes
Point Reyes Alert	38.101	-122.930	53	COOP	2/2/1993	Present	Yes
Point Reyes Light Stn.	38.000	-123.017	88	COOP	1/1/1899	Present	Yes
Pt. Reyes Lighthouse	37.996	-123.021	160	DRI	10/1/2006	Present	Yes
Pt. Reyes RCA	38.094	-122.950	27	DRI	10/1/2006	Present	Yes
Point Reyes R.S.	38.123	-122.908	76	GPMP	11/1/1987	12/31/1992	Yes
Olema Valley	38.043	-122.796	11	RAWS	5/1/2005	Present	Yes
Point Reyes Light Stn.	38.000	-123.017	88	SAO	1/1/1899	Present	Yes
BAMI6	37.950	-122.400	111	BAMI	M	Present	No
Fort Funston	37.713	-122.499	17	CARB	M	Present	No
Mount Tamalpais	37.926	-122.587	232	CARB	M	Present	No
Richmond-7th Street	37.948	-122.365	11	CARB	M	Present	No
San Fran Sewage Treat. Plt.	37.739	-122.390	2	CARB	M	Present	No
San Francisco-Hunters Point	37.734	-122.383	250	CARB	M	Present	No
San Pablo - El Portal	37.963	-122.340	15	CARB	M	Present	No
San Pablo-Rumrill Blvd.	37.960	-122.356	9	CARB	M	Present	No
Santa Rosa	38.444	-122.709	49	CARB	M	Present	No
Valley Ford	38.307	-122.896	5	CARB	M	Present	No
Bennett Valley	38.419	-122.657	82	CIMIS	10/1/2000	Present	No
Black Point	38.091	-122.527	0	CIMIS	6/1/2003	Present	No
Novato	38.121	-122.543	8	CIMIS	7/1/1986	1/31/2002	No
Petaluma East	38.267	-122.616	30	CIMIS	8/1/1999	Present	No
Point San Pedro	37.992	-122.470	2	CIMIS	12/1/2002	Present	No
Santa Rosa	38.401	-122.796	24	CIMIS	1/1/1990	Present	No
Valley of the Moon	38.312	-122.499	47	CIMIS	M	Present	No
Windsor	38.526	-122.833	26	CIMIS	12/1/1990	Present	No
Berkeley	37.874	-122.259	94	COOP	1/1/1893	Present	No
Cazadero	38.533	-123.133	323	COOP	11/10/1939	9/1/1971	No
Cazadero 5 NW	38.564	-123.162	433	COOP	9/1/1971	Present	No
Crissy Field	37.800	-122.467	2	COOP	5/1/1928	6/30/1936	No
Fort Point	37.800	-122.467	3	COOP	3/1/1951	3/2/2000	No
Fort Ross	38.515	-123.245	34	COOP	10/1/1895	Present	No
Graton	38.431	-122.865	61	COOP	1/1/1926	Present	No
Guerneville	38.504	-122.997	18	COOP	11/8/1939	Present	No
Guerneville Fire Dept.	38.504	-122.997	20	COOP	4/1/1971	9/13/2005	No

Name	Lat.	Lon.	Elev. (m)	Network	Start	End	In Park?
Hacienda Bridge	38.509	-122.927	6	COOP	6/1/1957	8/11/2004	No
Hamilton AFB	38.067	-122.517	4	COOP	2/1/1934	1/31/1976	No
Hamilton AFB 1 E	38.050	-122.500	3	COOP	5/1/1955	8/31/1959	No
Kentfield	37.957	-122.544	44	COOP	1/1/1902	Present	No
Mount Tamalpais	37.917	-122.583	793	COOP	12/1/1956	Present	No
Mount Tamalpais 2 SW	37.903	-122.603	447	COOP	2/1/1898	Present	No
Muir Woods	37.898	-122.569	67	COOP	12/1/1940	Present	No
Novato 8 WNW	38.133	-122.717	122	COOP	7/1/1948	10/23/1996	No
Oakland City Hall	37.800	-122.267	11	COOP	5/1/1949	11/30/1954	No
Oakland Light Stn.	37.800	-122.317	0	COOP	M	Present	No
Oakland Museum	37.798	-122.264	9	COOP	10/1/1970	Present	No
Occidental	38.386	-122.966	264	COOP	5/1/1940	Present	No
Pacifica	37.611	-122.484	38	COOP	9/22/2000	Present	No
Pacifica 4 SSE	37.592	-122.472	145	COOP	7/1/1983	Present	No
Petaluma	38.258	-122.608	6	COOP	2/1/1893	Present	No
Petaluma 1 N	38.250	-122.633	9	COOP	7/1/1948	6/30/1964	No
Point Reyes Stn.	38.067	-122.800	9	COOP	1/1/1931	4/30/1936	No
Richmond	37.919	-122.377	6	COOP	12/1/1950	Present	No
Richmond Field Stn.	37.917	-122.333	3	COOP	8/1/1955	9/30/1959	No
S E Farallon	37.700	-123.000	12	COOP	4/1/1903	Present	No
San Francisco	37.769	-122.433	53	COOP	10/1/1849	Present	No
San Francisco Acad. O.	37.767	-122.467	76	COOP	7/1/1951	8/31/1957	No
San Francisco Intl. Arpt.	37.658	-122.438	2	COOP	5/1/1928	Present	No
San Francisco Oceans	37.728	-122.504	2	COOP	7/1/1948	Present	No
San Rafael Civic Center	37.998	-122.537	37	COOP	1/1/1894	Present	No
Santa Rosa	38.438	-122.698	53	COOP	6/1/1902	Present	No
Santa Rosa	38.504	-122.810	35	COOP	4/1/1943	Present	No
Santa Rosa R.S.	38.450	-122.767	31	COOP	4/1/1953	Present	No
Sausalito	37.850	-122.483	0	COOP	1/1/1904	6/30/1914	No
Sebastopol	38.409	-122.821	21	COOP	7/1/1948	Present	No
Sonoma	38.299	-122.462	30	COOP	1/1/1893	Present	No
Woodacre	37.983	-122.583	128	COOP	4/1/1953	Present	No
AD6WX Mill Valley	37.886	-122.532	107	CWOP	M	Present	No
CW0013 Inverness	38.073	-122.844	290	CWOP	M	Present	No
CW0211 Sebastopol	38.440	-122.869	37	CWOP	M	Present	No
CW0677 Santa Rosa	38.452	-122.758	32	CWOP	M	Present	No
CW0879 Hercules	38.007	-122.277	42	CWOP	M	Present	No
CW0888 Pacifica	37.647	-122.474	207	CWOP	M	Present	No
CW0963 Daly City	37.667	-122.488	153	CWOP	M	Present	No
CW1655 Windsor	38.549	-122.798	38	CWOP	M	Present	No
CW1751 San Francisco	37.780	-122.476	30	CWOP	M	Present	No
CW2038 Windsor	38.549	-122.798	38	CWOP	M	Present	No
CW2054 Pacifica	37.638	-122.494	25	CWOP	M	Present	No
CW3537 Novato	38.084	-122.568	15	CWOP	M	Present	No
CW3602 San Rafael	37.997	-122.467	20	CWOP	M	Present	No
CW3627 Sabastopol	38.402	-122.828	44	CWOP	M	Present	No

Name	Lat.	Lon.	Elev. (m)	Network	Start	End	In Park?
CW3628 Santa Rosa	38.445	-122.706	60	CWOP	M	Present	No
CW3724 Sebastopol	38.411	-122.842	56	CWOP	M	Present	No
CW3741 Occidental	38.437	-122.974	46	CWOP	M	Present	No
CW3879 El Sobrante	37.976	-122.305	99	CWOP	M	Present	No
CW4081 Occidental	38.439	-122.976	650	CWOP	M	Present	No
CW4478 Petaluma	38.238	-122.601	8	CWOP	M	Present	No
CW5786 Santa Rosa	38.419	-122.752	40	CWOP	M	Present	No
CW5813 Guerneville	38.498	-123.002	53	CWOP	M	Present	No
KA6TGI Daly City	37.705	-122.430	177	CWOP	M	Present	No
KE6FWD Mill Valley	37.908	-122.576	294	CWOP	M	Present	No
KF6TYS Guerneville	38.512	-122.999	19	CWOP	M	Present	No
KF6YUA Sebastopol	38.380	-122.824	70	CWOP	M	Present	No
N6WKZ San Francisco	37.752	-122.453	200	CWOP	M	Present	No
WA6LCN Marinwood	38.030	-122.545	40	CWOP	M	Present	No
WW6HAM Pacifica	37.645	-122.472	195	CWOP	M	Present	No
Bodega Bay	38.320	-123.070	15	GPS-MET	M	Present	No
Barnaby	38.028	-122.702	378	RAWS	1/1/1997	Present	No
Big Rock	38.039	-122.570	457	RAWS	9/1/2003	Present	No
Golden Gate NRA #1	37.833	-122.535	457	RAWS	7/1/1995	11/30/1999	No
Middle Peak	37.931	-122.591	759	RAWS	5/1/2004	Present	No
Santa Rosa	38.479	-122.712	171	RAWS	3/1/1991	Present	No
Woodacre	37.991	-122.645	427	RAWS	5/1/2003	Present	No
Alameda	37.733	-122.317	5	SAO	7/1/1941	Present	No
Bodega Bay Station	38.317	-123.050	3	SAO	4/8/1971	Present	No
Crissy	37.800	-122.467	6	SAO	12/1/1922	4/30/1936	No
Farallon	37.700	-123.000	9	SAO	12/1/1943	12/31/1945	No
Hamilton AFB	38.067	-122.517	4	SAO	2/1/1934	1/31/1976	No
Point Blunt Sausalito	37.850	-122.417	73	SAO	10/1/1972	Present	No
Point Bonita Sausalito	37.817	-122.533	1	SAO	9/1/1972	Present	No
S E Farallon	37.700	-123.000	12	SAO	4/1/1903	Present	No
San Francisco Intl. Arpt.	37.658	-122.438	2	SAO	5/1/1928	Present	No
San Francisco PBS	37.750	-122.683	5	SAO	11/1/1973	Present	No
Santa Rosa	38.504	-122.810	35	SAO	4/1/1943	Present	No
Jenner	38.450	-123.133	72	WBAN	6/1/1943	12/31/1947	No
Monte Rio	38.500	-123.000	0	WBAN	5/1/1944	9/30/1944	No
Mount Tamalpais	37.900	-122.583	290	WBAN	7/1/1940	10/31/1957	No
Mount Tamalpais	37.933	-122.583	724	WBAN	11/1/1898	2/28/1955	No
Oakland	37.800	-122.350	5	WBAN	1/1/1943	6/30/1943	No
San Francisco	37.783	-122.317	5	WBAN	10/1/1931	12/31/1933	No
San Pablo	37.983	-122.350	79	WBAN	5/1/1928	3/31/1939	No
San Rafael Hamilton	38.050	-122.500	1	WBAN	5/1/1935	5/31/1947	No
Santa Rosa	38.417	-122.750	42	WBAN	5/1/1943	12/31/1951	No
Vallejo	38.000	-122.333	14	WBAN	7/1/1942	8/31/1943	No
Corte Madera	37.930	-122.520	3	WX4U	M	Present	No
Downtown Santa Rosa	38.440	-122.710	61	WX4U	M	Present	No
Occidental	38.370	-123.000	223	WX4U	M	Present	No

Name	Lat.	Lon.	Elev. (m)	Network	Start	End	In Park?
Pickles Central San Rafael	37.980	-122.520	54	WX4U	M	Present	No
Rohnert Park	38.329	-122.681	46	WX4U	M	Present	No
Santa Rosa	38.450	-122.720	46	WX4U	M	Present	No
Sebastopol	38.370	-122.820	61	WX4U	M	Present	No

end of the south unit of GOGA. Only one of the three COOP stations we identified in GOGA is indicated to be active. This climate station, "Mount Tamalpais 2 SW," is located in the northern unit of GOGA, in Marin County, and has been active since 1898. Unfortunately, the data record at this station is unreliable. A CWOP station (Mill Valley) provides near-real-time data in the northern unit of GOGA. Two active RAWS weather stations were identified within GOGA and also provide near-real-time data in the park unit. The station "Pulgas" is located in the southern unit of GOGA (Figure 4.2), just west of San Carlos, has been operating since 1997. The data record for "Pulgas" has gaps from February to June of 2005, November and December of 2005, and January through March of 2006. The RAWS station "Spring Valley" is also located in the southern unit of GOGA. "Spring Valley" has been active since 1998 and has a very complete data record. Two SAO stations provide near-real-time data within the northern unit of GOGA (Figure 4.1). These two stations are located at Points Blunt and Bonita, near the town of Sausalito. The WX4U station "Burlingame" is located in the southern unit of GOGA.

Of the 46 COOP stations we identified within 20 km of GOGA (Table 4.3), 28 are active. The COOP station "San Francisco," located at Mission Delores in downtown San Francisco (see Figure 4.2), is 3 km south of the closest boundary of GOGA and provides the longest climate record in the area (1849-present). This climate station provides a very reliable data record. Several other COOP stations in the area have data records that go back to the 1890s, with varying degrees of reliability. The COOP station "Berkeley" is 14 km east of GOGA and has a data record which goes back to 1893. This data record had a significant gap from January 1991 to November 1993 but is otherwise largely complete. The COOP station "San Rafael Civic Center" has been operating since 1894 and is 9 km north of the Marin County unit of GOGA. This climate station's data record was quite unreliable before 1948, with only sporadic data. After 1948, this site has been fairly reliable, although a significant gap occurred from January 1981 through April 1984. The COOP station "Point Reyes Light Stn." is 18 km northwest of the Marin County unit of GOGA. This station's data record goes back to 1899; unfortunately, this data record is unreliable. The COOP station "Kentfield" has been operating since 1902 and is 4 km north of GOGA. This climate station's data record is largely complete, with only scattered, small data gaps. The COOP station "Redwood City" (1906-present) has had a reliable data record since October 1930. This station is 4 km east of the south unit of GOGA. San Francisco International Airport operates a COOP station (along with a SAO station) 3 km east of the south unit of GOGA. These climate records go back to 1928 and are generally very reliable. In contrast to this, the COOP and SAO stations at Oakland International Airport have had unreliable data records since 1983. Both of these records started in 1928. Several other active COOP stations within 20 km of GOGA have data records that go back to the 1940s or earlier.

Eight RAWS stations were identified within 20 km of GOGA (Table 4.3). Most of these stations have at least a few gaps in their data records. The longest record was found at "La Honda,"

Figure 4.1. Station locations for the SFAN park units in the north Bay Area.

Figure 4.2. Station locations for the SFAN park units in the south Bay Area.

which is 16 km south of the south unit of GOGA (Figure 4.2) and has been active since May 1990. This station had a gap in its data record in January 2006. The RAWS stations "Barnaby," "Middle Peak," and "Olema Valley" are all within a kilometer of the boundary of the northern unit of GOGA (Figure 4.1). "Barnaby" has been operating the longest of these three stations, having been active since 1997. A gap occurred in the data record of "Barnaby" from January through May of 2002. The RAWS station "Oakland North" is 17 km east of the north unit of GOGA and has been active since 1992. A data gap occurred at this site between March and June of 2006. The RAWS stations "Los Altos," 15 km southeast of the south unit of GOGA, has a data record that goes back to 1998. No data are available at this site for November and December of 2006.

We identified nine active SAO sites within 20 km of the boundaries of GOGA units (Table 4.3). In addition to the SAO stations at the San Francisco and Oakland International Airports, the SAO station "Palo Alto" has been active since 1928. This station is 14 km east of the south unit of GOGA (Figure 4.2) and has taken observations fairly reliably since November 2003. The SAO station "Alameda" is 12 km east of the north unit of GOGA (Figure 4.1). The data record at "Alameda" goes back to 1941 but has been unreliable since January 1997. Numerous CWOP and WX4U stations also provide near-real-time data within 20 km of GOGA.

Only one station has been identified within the boundaries of MUWO (Table 4.3). This is a WBAN station (Mount Tamalpais) that is no longer active. The closest active stations to MUWO are COOP stations. Two COOP stations ("Mount Tamalpais 2 SW" and "Muir Woods") are located within a kilometer of MUWO. While the data record at "Mount Tamalpais 2 SW" is generally unreliable, the data record of Muir Woods (1940-present) is largely complete, with some notable gaps in the 1980s. These gaps occurred from November 1986 through April 1987 and from November through December of 1987. This site measures precipitation only. Of the 16 COOP stations we identified within 20 km of MUWO, nine are active. The COOP station "San Francisco" (1849-present), discussed previously, is 18 km southeast of MUWO. The COOP station "San Rafael Civic Center" (1894-present), discussed previously, is 11 km northeast of MUWO. The COOP station "San Francisco Oceans" is located 19 km south of MUWO and has a data record that goes back to 1948. This record has been largely complete since 1958, with scattered, small data gaps.

Four active RAWS weather stations were identified within 20 km of MUWO (Table 4.3). The longest record was found at "Barnaby," discussed previously. This station is 17 km northwest of MUWO (Figure 4.1). The RAWS station "Big Rock" is 15 km north of MUWO. Its data record, which goes back to 2003, has a gap from January through March of 2005. "Middle Peak" is 3 km north of MUWO. This station's data record (2004-present) was quite reliable until December 2005. The RAWS station "Woodacre" is located 11 km north of MUWO and has been active since 2003. A gap occurred at this station from February through April of 2005.

Three active SAO stations were identified within 20 km of the boundaries of MUWO (Table 4.3). The closest SAO site to MUWO is at Point Bonita, near Sausalito. This SAO station is 8 km southeast of MUWO. Several CWOP and WX4U stations also provide near-real-time data within 20 km of MUWO.

Eight weather and climate stations were identified in PORE (Table 4.3; Figure 4.1). Only one of these stations is no longer active. The non-active station is a GPMP site (Point Reyes R.S.) that operated from 1987 to 1992. A CARB station (Point Reyes Natl. Seashore) currently operates in the north-central portion of the park unit (Figure 4.1). Two active COOP stations were identified within PORE. "Point Reyes Light Stn." has been discussed previously, along with the collocated SAO station of the same name. The COOP station "Point Reyes Alert" has been operating in PORE since 1993. Two DRI stations provide near-real-time weather data within PORE. One of these stations operates at the Point Reyes Lighthouse, while the other station, "Pt. Reyes RCA," is located in the west-central part of the park unit. The RAWS station "Olema Valley," discussed previously, is in eastern PORE.

Besides the CARB station inside PORE, we have identified nine active CARB stations within 40 km of the park unit (Table 4.3). Most of these are located south and east of PORE (Figure 4.1). Eight CIMIS stations are active within 40 km of PORE. The closest CIMIS station to PORE is "Point San Pedro," which is 22 km east of the park unit. This station has been active since 2002.

Of the 41 COOP stations we identified within 40 km of PORE (Table 4.3), 27 are active. The COOP station "San Francisco," discussed previously, provides the longest data record among all these active COOP stations and is 28 km southeast of PORE. Several other COOP stations in the area have data records that go back to the 1890s, with varying degrees of reliability. The COOP stations "Berkeley" (39 km southeast of PORE), "Mount Tamalpais 2 SW" (9 km east), and "San Rafael Civic Center" (16 km east) have both been discussed previously. The COOP station "Petaluma" has been operating since 1893 and is 28 km northeast of PORE. This station's data record was quite sporadic until 1927, after which it has been largely complete. Notable gaps occurred at "Petaluma" in both 1990 (August; October through December) and 1991 (August through December). The COOP station "Sonoma" (1893-present) is 40 km northeast of PORE. This station's data record is quite sporadic before 1952. Since that time, the record has been largely complete, although a significant gap occurred between March and July of 1985. The COOP station "Fort Ross" (1895-present) is 37 km northwest of PORE. Until 1948, this station measured precipitation primarily. This station's data record is fairly complete, with only scattered, small data gaps. The COOP station "Kentfield," discussed previously, is 14 km east of PORE. The COOP station "Santa Rosa" (1902-present) is 34 km northeast of PORE. This station's data record had a large gap from February through June of 1979 but is otherwise very complete. The COOP station "S E Farallon" is located off the Pacific coast, 32 km south of PORE. This station is indicated to have been active since 1903 but its data record is not reliable. Two COOP stations of note have very reliable data records. "Graton" (1926-present) is located 24 km north of PORE, while "San Francisco Intl. Arpt." (discussed previously) is 36 km southeast of PORE. Several other active COOP stations within 20 km of GOGA have data records that go back to the 1940s or earlier.

A GPS-MET station at Bodega Bay, 10 km northwest of PORE (Figure 4.1), provides near-real-time weather data. Numerous CWOP and WX4U stations also provide near-real-time data within 40 km of PORE (Table 4.3). In addition to these stations, we have identified at least five active RAWS stations and eight active SAO stations that provide near-real-time data within 40 km of PORE. The RAWS stations "Barnaby" and "Woodacre," discussed previously, are 6 and 7 km east of PORE, respectively. The RAWS stations "Big Rock" and "Middle Peak," also discussed previously, are 16 and 10 km east of PORE, respectively. The RAWS station "Santa Rosa" is 37 km northeast of PORE and provides a reliable data record which goes back to 1991, making it the oldest active RAWS station among those identified for PORE. The SAO station "Santa Rosa" is 33 km northeast of PORE. Data have been reliable from this site since October 2003. The most reliable SAO record comes from San Francisco International Airport; however, this station is 36 km southeast of PORE.

4.2.2. South Bay Area

No weather or climate stations were identified within the boundaries of FOPO (Table 4.4). The closest active station to FOPO is the CWOP station "CW1751 San Francisco," which is 3 km south of the park unit. Several other CWOP stations in the area also provide near-real-time weather data. Six CARB stations were identified within 20 km of FOPO. The closest CARB stations to FOPO ("Fort Funston" and "San Francisco-Hunters Point") are located 11 km to the south of the park unit (Figure 4.2). Other sources of near-real-time weather data come from RAWS and SAO stations. The RAWS station "Middle Peak," discussed previously, is 17 km northwest of FOPO. The closest SAO to FOPO is "Point Bonita Sausalito" (1972-present), located only 5 km northwest of the park unit. The SAO at San Francisco International Airport provides the longest SAO record within 20 km of FOPO.

Out of the 17 COOP stations identified within 20 km of the boundaries of FOPO, 11 are active (Table 4.4). The longest record we identified was from the COOP station "San Francisco," discussed previously. This climate station is also the closest active COOP station to FOPO, being only 5 km southeast of the park unit. A few other COOP stations within 20 km of FOPO have data records going back to the 1890s. "Berkeley" (20 km northeast of FOPO) and "Mount Tamalpais 2 SW" (15 km northwest of FOPO) were discussed previously. Another long-term record for FOPO is found at "Kentfield" (17 km north), discussed previously. The COOP station "San Francisco Intl. Arpt." provides a reliable long-term record 17 km south of FOPO. Several other COOP stations we identified have data records going back to the 1950s or earlier.

Table 4.4. Weather and climate stations for the SFAN park units in the south Bay Area. Stations inside park units and within 20 km of the park unit boundary are included. Missing entries are indicated by "M".

Name	Lat.	Lon.	Elev. (m)	Network	Start	End	In Park?
Fort Point National Historic Site (FOPO)							
BAMI6	37.950	-122.400	111	BAMI	M	Present	No
Fort Funston	37.713	-122.499	17	CARB	M	Present	No
Mount Tamalpais	37.926	-122.587	232	CARB	M	Present	No
Richmond-7th Street	37.948	-122.365	11	CARB	M	Present	No
San Fran Sewage Treat. Plt.	37.739	-122.390	2	CARB	M	Present	No
San Francisco-Hunters Point	37.734	-122.383	250	CARB	M	Present	No
San Pablo-Rumrill Blvd.	37.960	-122.356	9	CARB	M	Present	No
Point San Pedro	37.992	-122.470	2	CIMIS	12/1/2002	Present	No
Berkeley	37.874	-122.259	94	COOP	1/1/1893	Present	No
Crissy Field	37.800	-122.467	2	COOP	5/1/1928	6/30/1936	No
Fort Point	37.800	-122.467	3	COOP	3/1/1951	3/2/2000	No
Kentfield	37.957	-122.544	44	COOP	1/1/1902	Present	No
Mount Tamalpais	37.917	-122.583	793	COOP	12/1/1956	Present	No
Mount Tamalpais 2 SW	37.903	-122.603	447	COOP	2/1/1898	Present	No

Name	Lat.	Lon.	Elev. (m)	Network	Start	End	In Park?
Muir Woods	37.898	-122.569	67	COOP	12/1/1940	Present	No
Oakland City Hall	37.800	-122.267	11	COOP	5/1/1949	11/30/1954	No
Oakland Light Stn.	37.800	-122.317	0	COOP	M	Present	No
Oakland Museum	37.798	-122.264	9	COOP	10/1/1970	Present	No
Richmond	37.919	-122.377	6	COOP	12/1/1950	Present	No
Richmond Field Stn.	37.917	-122.333	3	COOP	8/1/1955	9/30/1959	No
San Francisco	37.769	-122.433	53	COOP	10/1/1849	Present	No
San Francisco Acad. O.	37.767	-122.467	76	COOP	7/1/1951	8/31/1957	No
San Francisco Intl. Arpt.	37.658	-122.438	2	COOP	5/1/1928	Present	No
San Francisco Oceans	37.728	-122.504	2	COOP	7/1/1948	Present	No
Sausalito	37.850	-122.483	0	COOP	1/1/1904	6/30/1914	No
AD6WX Mill Valley	37.886	-122.532	107	CWOP	M	Present	No
CW0888 Pacifica	37.647	-122.474	207	CWOP	M	Present	No
CW0963 Daly City	37.667	-122.488	153	CWOP	M	Present	No
CW1751 San Francisco	37.780	-122.476	30	CWOP	M	Present	No
CW2054 Pacifica	37.638	-122.494	25	CWOP	M	Present	No
KA6TGI Daly City	37.705	-122.430	177	CWOP	M	Present	No
KE6FWD Mill Valley	37.908	-122.576	294	CWOP	M	Present	No
N6WKZ San Francisco	37.752	-122.453	200	CWOP	M	Present	No
WW6HAM Pacifica	37.645	-122.472	195	CWOP	M	Present	No
Golden Gate NRA #1	37.833	-122.535	457	RAWS	7/1/1995	11/30/1999	No
Middle Peak	37.931	-122.591	759	RAWS	5/1/2004	Present	No
Alameda	37.733	-122.317	5	SAO	7/1/1941	Present	No
Crissy	37.800	-122.467	6	SAO	12/1/1922	4/30/1936	No
Point Blunt Sausalito	37.850	-122.417	73	SAO	10/1/1972	Present	No
Point Bonita Sausalito	37.817	-122.533	1	SAO	9/1/1972	Present	No
San Francisco Intl. Arpt.	37.658	-122.438	2	SAO	5/1/1928	Present	No
San Francisco PBS	37.750	-122.683	5	SAO	11/1/1973	Present	No
Mount Tamalpais	37.900	-122.583	290	WBAN	7/1/1940	10/31/1957	No
Mount Tamalpais	37.933	-122.583	724	WBAN	11/1/1898	2/28/1955	No
Oakland	37.800	-122.350	5	WBAN	1/1/1943	6/30/1943	No
San Francisco	37.783	-122.317	5	WBAN	10/1/1931	12/31/1933	No
Corte Madera	37.930	-122.520	3	WX4U	M	Present	No
Pickles Central San Rafael	37.980	-122.520	54	WX4U	M	Present	No

Presidio of San Francisco (PRSF)

Name	Lat.	Lon.	Elev. (m)	Network	Start	End	In Park?
Crissy Field	37.800	-122.467	2	COOP	5/1/1928	6/30/1936	Yes
Fort Point	37.800	-122.467	3	COOP	3/1/1951	3/2/2000	Yes
Crissy	37.800	-122.467	6	SAO	12/1/1922	4/30/1936	Yes
BAMI6	37.950	-122.400	111	BAMI	M	Present	No
Fort Funston	37.713	-122.499	17	CARB	M	Present	No
Mount Tamalpais	37.926	-122.587	232	CARB	M	Present	No
Richmond-7th Street	37.948	-122.365	11	CARB	M	Present	No
San Fran Sewage Treat. Plt.	37.739	-122.390	2	CARB	M	Present	No
San Francisco-Hunters Point	37.734	-122.383	250	CARB	M	Present	No
San Pablo - El Portal	37.963	-122.340	15	CARB	M	Present	No
San Pablo-Rumrill Blvd.	37.960	-122.356	9	CARB	M	Present	No

Name	Lat.	Lon.	Elev. (m)	Network	Start	End	In Park?
Point San Pedro	37.992	-122.470	2	CIMIS	12/1/2002	Present	No
Berkeley	37.874	-122.259	94	COOP	1/1/1893	Present	No
Kentfield	37.957	-122.544	44	COOP	1/1/1902	Present	No
Mount Tamalpais	37.917	-122.583	793	COOP	12/1/1956	Present	No
Mount Tamalpais 2 SW	37.903	-122.603	447	COOP	2/1/1898	Present	No
Muir Woods	37.898	-122.569	67	COOP	12/1/1940	Present	No
Oakland City Hall	37.800	-122.267	11	COOP	5/1/1949	11/30/1954	No
Oakland Light Stn.	37.800	-122.317	0	COOP	M	Present	No
Oakland Museum	37.798	-122.264	9	COOP	10/1/1970	Present	No
Pacifica	37.611	-122.484	38	COOP	9/22/2000	Present	No
Richmond	37.919	-122.377	6	COOP	12/1/1950	Present	No
Richmond Field Stn.	37.917	-122.333	3	COOP	8/1/1955	9/30/1959	No
San Francisco	37.769	-122.433	53	COOP	10/1/1849	Present	No
San Francisco Acad. O.	37.767	-122.467	76	COOP	7/1/1951	8/31/1957	No
San Francisco Intl. Arpt.	37.658	-122.438	2	COOP	5/1/1928	Present	No
San Francisco Oceans	37.728	-122.504	2	COOP	7/1/1948	Present	No
Sausalito	37.850	-122.483	0	COOP	1/1/1904	6/30/1914	No
AD6WX Mill Valley	37.886	-122.532	107	CWOP	M	Present	No
CW0277 Alameda	37.759	-122.238	2	CWOP	M	Present	No
CW0888 Pacifica	37.647	-122.474	207	CWOP	M	Present	No
CW0963 Daly City	37.667	-122.488	153	CWOP	M	Present	No
CW1634 Berkeley	37.856	-122.244	110	CWOP	M	Present	No
CW1751 San Francisco	37.780	-122.476	30	CWOP	M	Present	No
CW2054 Pacifica	37.638	-122.494	25	CWOP	M	Present	No
KA6TGI Daly City	37.705	-122.430	177	CWOP	M	Present	No
KE6FWD Mill Valley	37.908	-122.576	294	CWOP	M	Present	No
N6WKZ San Francisco	37.752	-122.453	200	CWOP	M	Present	No
WW6HAM Pacifica	37.645	-122.472	195	CWOP	M	Present	No
Golden Gate NRA #1	37.833	-122.535	457	RAWS	7/1/1995	11/30/1999	No
Middle Peak	37.931	-122.591	759	RAWS	5/1/2004	Present	No
Alameda	37.733	-122.317	5	SAO	7/1/1941	Present	No
Point Blunt Sausalito	37.850	-122.417	73	SAO	10/1/1972	Present	No
Point Bonita Sausalito	37.817	-122.533	1	SAO	9/1/1972	Present	No
San Francisco Intl. Arpt.	37.658	-122.438	2	SAO	5/1/1928	Present	No
San Francisco PBS	37.750	-122.683	5	SAO	11/1/1973	Present	No
Mount Tamalpais	37.900	-122.583	290	WBAN	7/1/1940	10/31/1957	No
Mount Tamalpais	37.933	-122.583	724	WBAN	11/1/1898	2/28/1955	No
Oakland	37.800	-122.350	5	WBAN	1/1/1943	6/30/1943	No
San Francisco	37.783	-122.317	5	WBAN	10/1/1931	12/31/1933	No
Corte Madera	37.930	-122.520	3	WX4U	M	Present	No
Pickles Central San Rafael	37.980	-122.520	54	WX4U	M	Present	No

Three stations were identified within PRSF (Table 4.4). However, none of these stations are active currently. The closest active station to PRSF is the CWOP station "CW1751 San Francisco," which is within a kilometer of the park unit. Several other CWOP stations in the area also provide near-real-time weather data. Seven CARB stations were identified within 20 km of FOPO. The closest CARB station to PRSF is "San Fran Sewage Treat. Plt.," which is located 8 km southeast of the park unit (Figure 4.2). Other sources of near-real-time weather data come from RAWS and SAO stations in the area. The RAWS station "Middle Peak," discussed previously, is 17 km northwest of PRSF. The SAO at San Francisco International Airport provides the longest and most reliable SAO record within 20 km of PRSF.

Out of the 16 COOP stations that were identified within 20 km of the boundaries of PRSF, 12 are active (Table 4.4). The longest record we identified was from the COOP station "San Francisco," discussed previously. This climate station is also the closest active COOP station to PRSF, being only 3 km south of the park unit. A few other COOP stations within 20 km of PRSF have data records going back to the 1890s. "Berkeley" (18 km northeast of PRSF) and "Mount Tamalpais 2 SW" (15 km northwest of PRSF) were discussed previously. Another long-term record for PRSF is found at "Kentfield" (17 km northwest), discussed previously. The COOP station "San Francisco Intl. Arpt." provides a reliable long-term record 15 km southeast of PRSF. Several other COOP stations we identified have data records going back to the 1950s or earlier.

4.2.2. East Bay Area

No weather/climate stations were identified within the boundaries of EUON (Table 4.5). Five CARB stations are located within 20 km of EUON. The closest of these stations to EUON is "Concord-2956 A Treat Blvd", which is 12 km north of EUON (Figure 4.3). Of the four active CIMIS stations within 20 km of EUON, the closest is "Moraga," which is 9 km west of EUON.

We identified 32 COOP stations within 20 km of EUON (Table 4.5); however, only nine of these are still active. The closest active COOP station to EUON is "Mt. Diablo Junction," which is 10 km northeast of EUON. This climate station has a largely complete data record going back to 1953. Scattered, small data gaps have occurred throughout the record at "Mt. Diablo Junction." The COOP stations "Concord" and "Oakland" both have data records that go back to 1928, making them the longest records of the active COOP stations we identified for EUON. "Oakland" is 20 km west of EUON and, as previously discussed, has not been reliable since the early 1980s. "Concord," 18 km north of EUON, has produced data reliably since October 2003 but the data record has uncertain reliability before that time. The COOP station "Round Top" is 15 km west of EUON and has been operating since 1943. This station has been unreliable since 1960. The COOP station "Upper San Leandro Fltr." is 13 km southwest of EUON and has a data record which starts in 1948. This climate station has a large gap between October 1951 and July 1958. Between August 1958 and April 1990, no temperatures were measured at this station.

Table 4.5. Weather and climate stations for the SFAN park units in the east Bay Area. Stations inside park units and within 20 km of the park unit boundary are included. Missing entries are indicated by "M".

Name	Lat.	Lon.	Elev. (m)	Network	Start	End	In Park?
Eugene O'Neil National Historic Site (EUON)							
Chabot	37.719	-122.098	52	CARB	M	Present	No
Concord	37.939	-122.025	26	CARB	M	Present	No
Concord-2956 A Treat Blvd.	37.936	-122.030	27	CARB	M	Present	No
Kregor Peak	37.943	-122.095	176	CARB	M	Present	No
Pleasanton	37.697	-121.912	30	CARB	M	Present	No

Name	Lat.	Lon.	Elev. (m)	Network	Start	End	In Park?
Concord	38.004	-122.020	11	CIMIS	4/1/2001	Present	No
Moraga	37.838	-122.139	155	CIMIS	2/1/2002	Present	No
Oakland Foothills	37.781	-122.179	44	CIMIS	3/1/1999	Present	No
Walnut Creek	37.914	-122.082	134	CIMIS	M	Present	No
Alamo 1 N	37.867	-122.033	125	COOP	1/1/1956	7/1/1975	No
Burton Ranch	37.867	-122.083	162	COOP	8/1/1956	11/26/1974	No
Clayton 1 SW	37.933	-121.967	308	COOP	1/1/1956	6/30/1958	No
Concord	37.992	-122.055	5	COOP	6/1/1928	Present	No
Concord	37.967	-122.033	21	COOP	4/1/1953	Present	No
Concord 1 SE	37.967	-122.017	34	COOP	11/12/1954	6/30/1958	No
Concord 2 SE	37.950	-122.000	79	COOP	1/1/1956	9/30/1957	No
Concord 3 E	37.967	-121.983	59	COOP	11/24/1954	1/24/1975	No
Concord Airport	37.983	-122.017	6	COOP	12/1/1947	4/30/1950	No
Concord Waste Plant	37.983	-122.069	12	COOP	5/1/1971	Present	No
Haviside Ranch	37.950	-122.100	101	COOP	1/1/1956	6/30/1958	No
Hayward	37.654	-122.115	13	COOP	6/1/1955	Present	No
Hayward 4 ESE	37.667	-122.000	162	COOP	7/1/1948	5/20/1988	No
La Fayette Fire Stn.	37.883	-122.117	88	COOP	1/1/1956	6/30/1958	No
Lafayette 2 NNE	37.917	-122.100	165	COOP	12/3/1954	6/30/1977	No
Martinez 2 S	37.970	-122.128	70	COOP	7/1/1948	9/30/2005	No
Martinez 3 SSE	37.967	-122.100	79	COOP	1/1/1956	10/1/1975	No
Mt. Diablo Junction	37.879	-121.930	661	COOP	3/10/1952	Present	No
Mt. Diablo State Park	37.850	-121.933	488	COOP	1/1/1956	6/30/1958	No
Oakland	37.721	-122.221	2	COOP	5/1/1928	Present	No
Oakland	37.783	-122.167	134	COOP	10/4/1894	7/31/1958	No
Orinda	37.883	-122.200	113	COOP	5/1/1953	Present	No
Orinda Bowman	37.867	-122.167	168	COOP	8/1/1944	6/30/1960	No
Pleasant Hill 1 NW	37.950	-122.083	18	COOP	1/1/1956	6/30/1958	No
Round Top	37.850	-122.200	537	COOP	7/1/1943	Present	No
Saint Marys College	37.833	-122.100	189	COOP	12/1/1942	12/31/1980	No
San Ramon 1 SSW	37.767	-121.983	171	COOP	1/1/1956	6/30/1958	No
Upper San Leandro Fltr.	37.772	-122.168	120	COOP	7/1/1948	Present	No
Walmar School	37.950	-122.083	37	COOP	1/1/1956	10/3/1973	No
Walnut Creek 2 ENE	37.900	-122.017	67	COOP	7/1/1948	6/21/1983	No
Walnut Creek 2 ESE	37.883	-122.033	76	COOP	1/1/1893	1/24/1975	No
Walnut Creek 4 E	37.900	-121.983	122	COOP	1/1/1956	6/30/1977	No
CW0277 Alameda	37.759	-122.238	2	CWOP	M	Present	No
CW0519 Castro Valley	37.696	-122.100	100	CWOP	M	Present	No
CW0830 Walnut Creek	37.899	-122.051	49	CWOP	M	Present	No
CW1022 Clayton	37.927	-121.926	158	CWOP	M	Present	No
CW1176 Concord	37.952	-122.001	8	CWOP	M	Present	No
CW1634 Berkeley	37.856	-122.244	110	CWOP	M	Present	No
CW2655 Walnut Creek	37.921	-122.073	38	CWOP	M	Present	No
CW3130 Lafayette	37.894	-122.164	211	CWOP	M	Present	No
CW3190 Oakland	37.775	-122.138	244	CWOP	M	Present	No
CW3884 Concord	37.962	-122.008	24	CWOP	M	Present	No

Name	Lat.	Lon.	Elev. (m)	Network	Start	End	In Park?
CW4190 Dublin	37.725	-121.868	157	CWOP	M	Present	No
CW4622 Diablo	37.850	-121.953	260	CWOP	M	Present	No
CW4764 San Ramon	37.763	-121.978	158	CWOP	M	Present	No
CW4895 Martinez	38.007	-122.076	15	CWOP	M	Present	No
CW4937 Orinda	37.851	-122.168	225	CWOP	M	Present	No
CW5029 Lafayette	37.896	-122.136	222	CWOP	M	Present	No
K6BMD-9 Walnut Creek	37.916	-122.036	35	CWOP	M	Present	No
KF6IIU Lafayette	37.889	-122.108	122	CWOP	M	Present	No
Briones	37.944	-122.118	442	RAWS	4/1/1994	Present	No
Las Trampas	37.834	-122.067	536	RAWS	4/1/1994	Present	No
Mt. Diablo	37.867	-121.901	1173	RAWS	7/1/2000	Present	No
Oakland North	37.875	-122.217	152	RAWS	6/1/1992	Present	No
Oakland South	37.788	-122.162	0	RAWS	8/1/1992	Present	No
Concord	37.992	-122.055	5	SAO	6/1/1928	Present	No
Hayward	37.654	-122.115	13	SAO	6/1/1955	Present	No
Oakland	37.721	-122.221	2	SAO	5/1/1928	Present	No
Oakland	37.733	-122.200	2	SAO	6/1/1949	12/31/1961	No
Concord Muncheevil	37.960	-122.000	61	WX4U	M	Present	No
Dimond District Oakland	37.796	-122.208	52	WX4U	M	Present	No
Dublin	37.720	-121.940	137	WX4U	M	Present	No
Oakland	37.800	-122.210	122	WX4U	M	Present	No

John Muir National Historic Site (JOMU)

Name	Lat.	Lon.	Elev. (m)	Network	Start	End	In Park?
Concord	37.939	-122.025	26	CARB	M	Present	No
Concord-2956 A Treat Blvd	37.936	-122.030	27	CARB	M	Present	No
Kregor Peak	37.943	-122.095	176	CARB	M	Present	No
Richmond-7th Street	37.948	-122.365	11	CARB	M	Present	No
San Pablo - El Portal	37.963	-122.340	15	CARB	M	Present	No
San Pablo-Rumrill Blvd.	37.960	-122.356	9	CARB	M	Present	No
Vallejo	38.102	-122.238	30	CARB	M	Present	No
Concord	38.004	-122.020	11	CIMIS	4/1/2001	Present	No
Moraga	37.838	-122.139	155	CIMIS	2/1/2002	Present	No
Walnut Creek	37.914	-122.082	134	CIMIS	M	Present	No
Alamo 1 N	37.867	-122.033	125	COOP	1/1/1956	7/1/1975	No
Berkeley	37.874	-122.259	94	COOP	1/1/1893	Present	No
Burton Ranch	37.867	-122.083	162	COOP	8/1/1956	11/26/1974	No
Carquinez Bridge	38.067	-122.233	6	COOP	3/1/1929	Present	No
Clayton 1 SW	37.933	-121.967	308	COOP	1/1/1956	6/30/1958	No
Concord	37.992	-122.055	5	COOP	6/1/1928	Present	No
Concord	37.967	-122.033	21	COOP	4/1/1953	Present	No
Concord 1 SE	37.967	-122.017	34	COOP	11/12/1954	6/30/1958	No
Concord 2 SE	37.950	-122.000	79	COOP	1/1/1956	9/30/1957	No
Concord 3 E	37.967	-121.983	59	COOP	11/24/1954	1/24/1975	No
Concord Airport	37.983	-122.017	6	COOP	12/1/1947	4/30/1950	No
Concord Waste Plant	37.983	-122.069	12	COOP	5/1/1971	Present	No
Crockett	38.033	-122.217	3	COOP	1/1/1918	2/28/1977	No
Haviside Ranch	37.950	-122.100	101	COOP	1/1/1956	6/30/1958	No

Name	Lat.	Lon.	Elev. (m)	Network	Start	End	In Park?
La Fayette Fire Stn.	37.883	-122.117	88	COOP	1/1/1956	6/30/1958	No
Lafayette 2 NNE	37.917	-122.100	165	COOP	12/3/1954	6/30/1977	No
Mare Island	38.100	-122.267	15	COOP	1/1/1961	12/31/1975	No
Martinez 2 S	37.970	-122.128	70	COOP	7/1/1948	9/30/2005	No
Martinez 3 SSE	37.967	-122.100	79	COOP	1/1/1956	10/1/1975	No
Martinez Water Plant	38.013	-122.114	12	COOP	3/3/1906	Present	No
Mt. Diablo Junction	37.879	-121.930	661	COOP	3/10/1952	Present	No
Orinda	37.883	-122.200	113	COOP	5/1/1953	Present	No
Orinda Bowman	37.867	-122.167	168	COOP	8/1/1944	6/30/1960	No
Pleasant Hill 1 NW	37.950	-122.083	18	COOP	1/1/1956	6/30/1958	No
Port Chicago Naval D.	38.017	-122.017	15	COOP	4/1/1946	9/29/1975	No
Richmond Field Stn.	37.917	-122.333	3	COOP	8/1/1955	9/30/1959	No
Round Top	37.850	-122.200	537	COOP	7/1/1943	Present	No
Saint Marys College	37.833	-122.100	189	COOP	12/1/1942	12/31/1980	No
Vallejo	38.140	-122.234	40	COOP	9/1/1997	Present	No
Walmar School	37.950	-122.083	37	COOP	1/1/1956	10/3/1973	No
Walnut Creek 2 ENE	37.900	-122.017	67	COOP	7/1/1948	6/21/1983	No
Walnut Creek 2 ESE	37.883	-122.033	76	COOP	1/1/1893	1/24/1975	No
Walnut Creek 4 E	37.900	-121.983	122	COOP	1/1/1956	6/30/1977	No
CW0830 Walnut Creek	37.899	-122.051	49	CWOP	M	Present	No
CW0879 Hercules	38.007	-122.277	42	CWOP	M	Present	No
CW1022 Clayton	37.927	-121.926	158	CWOP	M	Present	No
CW1176 Concord	37.952	-122.001	8	CWOP	M	Present	No
CW1634 Berkeley	37.856	-122.244	110	CWOP	M	Present	No
CW2458 Vallejo	38.128	-122.194	127	CWOP	M	Present	No
CW2655 Walnut Creek	37.921	-122.073	38	CWOP	M	Present	No
CW3130 Lafayette	37.894	-122.164	211	CWOP	M	Present	No
CW3879 El Sobrante	37.976	-122.305	99	CWOP	M	Present	No
CW3884 Concord	37.962	-122.008	24	CWOP	M	Present	No
CW4895 Martinez	38.007	-122.076	15	CWOP	M	Present	No
CW4937 Orinda	37.851	-122.168	225	CWOP	M	Present	No
CW5029 Lafayette	37.896	-122.136	222	CWOP	M	Present	No
K6BMD-9 Walnut Creek	37.916	-122.036	35	CWOP	M	Present	No
K6TPK-11 No. Concord	38.029	-122.030	2	CWOP	M	Present	No
KF6IIU Lafayette	37.889	-122.108	122	CWOP	M	Present	No
WB6ABE-4 Benicia	38.078	-122.166	183	CWOP	M	Present	No
Briones	37.944	-122.118	442	RAWS	4/1/1994	Present	No
Las Trampas	37.834	-122.067	536	RAWS	4/1/1994	Present	No
Oakland North	37.875	-122.217	152	RAWS	6/1/1992	Present	No
Concord	37.992	-122.055	5	SAO	6/1/1928	Present	No
Concord PSS	38.050	-122.017	12	SAO	M	Present	No
Davis Point	38.050	-122.267	18	SAO	11/1/1973	Present	No
San Pablo	37.983	-122.350	79	WBAN	5/1/1928	3/31/1939	No
Vallejo	38.000	-122.333	14	WBAN	7/1/1942	8/31/1943	No
Concord Muncheevil	37.960	-122.000	61	WX4U	M	Present	No

Figure 4.3. Station locations for the SFAN park units in the east Bay Area.

We identified five RAWS stations that currently report near-real-time data within 20 km of EUON (Table 4.5). The closest RAWS station to EUON is "Las Trampas," which is 3 km west of the park unit (Figure 4.3). This station's data record, which goes back to 1994, has gaps in February-April 2000 and June 2001. The RAWS station with the longest data record is "Oakland North," which has been active since June 1992. This station is 17 km northwest of EUON. Its data record has a large gap in 2006 (March-June). "Oakland South" (12 km west of EUON) has been active since August 1992 but has several data gaps, including February 2005, June and July of 2006, and October 2006 through early 2007. The RAWS station "Briones" is 15 km northwest of EUON and has been active since 1994. Data gaps have occurred at this site in 2004 (August-November) and 2005 (January-February; May-July). The RAWS station "Mt. Diablo," which is 12 km northeast of EUON and has been active since 2000, has a very reliable data record.

Three active SAO stations were identified within 20 km of EUON (Table 4.5). The SAO stations "Oakland" has been discussed previously. The SAO station "Concord" is collocated with the aforementioned COOP station "Concord." The SAO station "Hayward" (1955-present) is 20 km southwest of EUON (Figure 4.3). This station has provided reliable data only since February 2003. In addition to the RAWS and SAO sites that were just discussed, numerous CWOP and WX4U stations provide near-real-time data within 20 km of EUON.

No weather or climate stations were identified within the boundaries of JOMU (Table 4.5). The closest active station to JOMU is the COOP station "Martinez Water Plant," which is 3 km northeast of the park unit. This station provides a long-term climate record (1906-present) which has been very complete since 1948. Seven CARB stations are located within 20 km of JOMU. The closest of these stations to JOMU is "Kregor Peak," which is 5 km southeast of JOMU (Figure 4.3). Of the three active CIMIS stations within 20 km of JOMU, the closest is "Walnut Creek," which is 8 km southeast of JOMU.

We identified 33 COOP stations within 20 km of JOMU (Table 4.5); however, only 10 of these are still active. The COOP station "Concord" (1928-present), discussed previously, is 6 km east of JOMU. The COOP station "Carquinez Bridge" (1929-present), 12 km northwest of JOMU, has an unreliable data record. The COOP station "Round Top," discussed previously, is 15 km southwest of JOMU. The COOP station "Mt. Diablo Junction," discussed previously, is 20 km southeast of JOMU and provides the only other reliable source of climate data we have identified for JOMU besides "Martinez Water Plant."

We identified three RAWS stations that currently report near-real-time data within 20 km of JOMU (Table 4.5). The closest RAWS station to JOMU is "Briones," which is 4 km south of the park unit (Figure 4.3). "Oakland North" is 14 km southwest of JOMU, while "Las Trampas" is 17 km southeast of JOMU.

Three active SAO stations were identified within 20 km of JOMU (Table 4.5). The SAO station "Concord" is the closest SAO station to JOMU, being located 6 km east of the park unit. "Concord PSS" is 12 km east of JOMU, while "Davis Point" is 13 km northwest of JOMU. In addition to the RAWS and SAO sites that were just discussed, numerous CWOP and WX4U stations provide near-real-time data within 20 km of JOMU.

4.2.2. Pinnacles National Monument

Six weather/climate stations were identified within the boundaries of PINN (Table 4.6; Figure 4.4). Only one of these stations is no longer active. The non-active station is a GPMP site (Pinnacles) that operated from 1987 to 1995. A CARB station (Pinnacles Natl. Monument) currently operates in the north-central portion of the park unit. A CASTNet station (Pinnacles NM) has been operating since 1987 in the east-central portion of the park unit, near the east entrance station. One active COOP station was identified within PINN. "Pinnacles NM" has been operating since 1937 near the Bear Gulch Visitor Center and has a fairly complete data record, with scattered, small data gaps. This station provides the primary climate record within PINN. The NADP station "Pinnacles NM-Bear Valley" has been operating since 1999 in east-central PINN. Finally, the RAWS station "Pinnacles" has been operating since 2001, also in east-central PINN, and has a very reliable record of near-real-time weather data.

Eight CIMIS stations (five active) were identified within 40 km of the boundaries of PINN (Table 4.6). The closest CIMIS station to PINN is "Arroyo Seco," which is 11 km southwest of PINN (Figure 4.4). This station has been active since 1993.

Out of the 23 COOP stations identified within 40 km of the boundaries of PINN, nine are active (Table 4.6). The longest record we identified was from the COOP station "Salinas," which is 35 km northwest of PINN. This station had numerous data gaps until 1931, at which point the data record has become very reliable. A SAO station (Salinas) is also located at this site. Another useful long-term record was identified at the COOP station "King City," which is 23 km south of PINN and has been active since 1902. The data record at "King City" has a large gap from January 1943 to March 1950 for temperature and from January 1943 to June 1948 for precipitation. Since those gaps, however, the data record has been fairly complete, with only scattered, small data gaps. The COOP station "Arroyo Seco" (1915-present) is 33 km southwest of PINN and measures precipitation only. This station's data record has been unreliable since 1954. The COOP station "Hernandez" (1939-present) is 31 km southeast of PINN. This station has an unreliable data record. "Paicines 4 W" is 21 km northwest of PINN and has a fairly complete data record that goes back to 1942. This station measured only precipitation until November 1993. The COOP station "Panoche 2 W" (23 km northeast of PINN) is a precipitation-only site that has been active since 1949. The data record at this station was very complete until July 2006.

Besides the CARB and CIMIS sites mentioned earlier, RAWS stations are the primary source of near-real-time data within 40 km of PINN (Table 4.6; Figure 4.4). Five RAWS stations were identified; four of these are active. The data records at these stations are quite complete, with the exception of "Hastings" (1997-present), which is 13 km northwest of PINN and has a data gap in June 2003. "Hernandez" (1990-present) is 26 km southeast of PINN. "Arroyo Seco (Mt. Diablo)" (1996-present) is 34 km southwest of PINN. "Hollister" (2002-present) is 33 km northwest of PINN.

Table 4.6. Weather and climate stations for PINN. Stations inside PINN and within 40 km of the PINN boundary are included. Missing entries are indicated by "M".

Pinnacles National Monument (PINN)

Name	Lat.	Lon.	Elev. (m)	Network	Start	End	In Park?
Pinnacles Natl. Monument	36.497	-121.172	335	CARB	M	Present	Yes
Pinnacles NM	36.485	-121.156	335	CASTNet	4/1/1987	Present	Yes
Pinnacles NM	36.482	-121.182	398	COOP	1/1/1937	Present	Yes
Pinnacles	36.485	-121.156	335	GPMP	4/1/1987	4/30/1995	Yes
Pinnacles NM-Bear Valley	36.482	-121.155	300	NADP	11/2/1999	Present	Yes
Pinnacles	36.471	-121.147	403	RAWS	3/1/2001	Present	Yes
Hollister-Fairview Rd.	36.843	-121.362	126	CARB	M	Present	No
King City-750 Metz Rd.	36.227	-121.115	93	CARB	M	Present	No
Arroyo Seco	36.359	-121.290	72	CIMIS	6/1/1993	Present	No
Gonzales	36.515	-121.510	45	CIMIS	6/1/1993	11/30/1998	No
Greenfield	36.341	-121.257	82	CIMIS	10/1/1986	10/31/1991	No
King City	36.174	-121.117	91	CIMIS	11/1/1982	12/31/1985	No
King City-Oasis Rd.	36.121	-121.084	165	CIMIS	6/1/1993	Present	No
Salinas South	36.610	-121.529	37	CIMIS	8/1/1992	Present	No
Soledad	36.447	-121.364	52	CIMIS	M	Present	No
USDA	36.620	-121.545	37	CIMIS	M	Present	No
Arroyo Seco	36.236	-121.480	287	COOP	1/1/1915	Present	No
Arroyo Seco Gauging	36.233	-121.483	244	COOP	6/1/1953	Present	No
Arroyo Seco Millers	36.250	-121.417	214	COOP	1/1/1949	12/31/1952	No
Arroyo Seco River	36.238	-121.481	245	COOP	1/1/1962	9/27/2004	No
Arroyo Seco Rock	36.233	-121.467	238	COOP	11/1/1954	10/31/1955	No
Buena Vista	36.767	-121.183	500	COOP	7/1/1948	7/1/1971	No
Chews Ridge Lookout	36.300	-121.567	1543	COOP	6/1/1953	Present	No
Gonzales 9 ENE	36.533	-121.283	717	COOP	7/1/1948	4/28/1976	No
Greenfield Groover Ranch	36.250	-121.433	0	COOP	7/1/1948	11/30/1948	No
Hernandez	36.367	-120.800	1202	COOP	12/1/1939	Present	No
Hernandez 2 NW	36.417	-120.917	659	COOP	5/1/1943	7/9/1980	No
King City	36.207	-121.138	98	COOP	6/16/1902	Present	No
King City Arpt.	36.233	-121.117	110	COOP	3/1/1940	4/30/1950	No
Mercey Hot Springs	36.700	-120.867	357	COOP	9/1/1932	12/1/1967	No
Paicines 4 W	36.716	-121.348	276	COOP	7/1/1942	Present	No
Paloma	36.350	-121.540	541	COOP	5/1/1940	4/5/1999	No
Panoche 2 W	36.607	-120.884	427	COOP	11/1/1949	Present	No
Salinas	36.659	-121.666	14	COOP	4/1/1958	Present	No
Salinas	36.664	-121.608	23	COOP	2/1/1878	Present	No
San Benito	36.509	-121.087	413	COOP	7/1/1948	8/1/2001	No
San Benito Willow Cr.	36.583	-121.183	299	COOP	2/1/1949	10/31/1955	No
Soledad	36.433	-121.317	64	COOP	3/1/1906	5/21/1984	No
Upper Tres Pinos	36.633	-121.033	616	COOP	7/1/1948	3/31/1977	No
KF6IHL-3 Moody Canyon	36.569	-120.961	659	CWOP	M	Present	No

Pinnacles National Monument (PINN)

Name	Lat.	Lon.	Elev. (m)	Network	Start	End	In Park?
WA6BAY-3 Mt. Toro	36.538	-121.626	945	CWOP	M	Present	No
Arroyo Seco (Mt. Diablo)	36.230	-121.492	299	RAWS	5/1/1996	Present	No
Cahoon	36.347	-121.511	683	RAWS	5/1/1990	4/30/1997	No
Hastings	36.551	-121.389	556	RAWS	4/1/1997	Present	No
Hernandez	36.383	-120.854	1144	RAWS	5/1/1990	Present	No
Hollister	36.842	-121.362	129	RAWS	12/1/2002	Present	No
Salinas	36.664	-121.608	23	SAO	2/1/1878	Present	No
King City	36.217	-121.133	117	WBAN	6/1/1928	4/30/1947	No
Salinas	36.667	-121.617	22	WBAN	8/1/1941	11/30/1945	No

Figure 4.4. Station locations for PINN.

49

5.0. Conclusions and Recommendations

We have based our findings on an examination of available climate records within SFAN units, discussions with NPS staff and other collaborators, and prior knowledge of the area. Here, we offer an evaluation and general comments pertaining to the status, prospects, and needs for climate-monitoring capabilities in SFAN.

5.1. San Francisco Bay Area Inventory and Monitoring Network

The SFAN network recognizes the need for improved weather and climate station coverage within its park units (NPS 2005). Weather and climate monitoring efforts at SFAN are already planning to maintain or establish several different types of climate and precipitation monitoring stations. Observations are desired that will represent a broad range of climate gradients in the SFAN, with the intent of collecting such observations for a number of years. Some of the SFAN park units, such as EUON, FOPO, JOMU, and PRSF, do not currently host any weather or climate stations. At these park units, SFAN plans to support data management at outside stations whose data are useful for park interests and represent the climate conditions, such as rainfall patterns, at these park units. Fortunately, the urban setting of much of the SFAN hosts a large number of potential outside sources of weather and climate data.

There are no reliable sources for long-term climate records for the SFAN park units in the San Francisco Bay Area. The long-term stations we identified in PORE (Point Reyes Light Stn.) and GOGA (Mount Tamalpais 2 SW) unfortunately do not have reliable data records. Therefore, these park units must rely on long-term climate records that exist outside of the park unit boundaries. Climate monitoring efforts by the NPS will benefit through the continued support of these valuable outside sources of climate data.

One such source of climate data is the COOP station "San Francisco," located at Mission Delores in downtown San Francisco. This station provides the longest reliable data record of all the climate records we identified for SFAN. One important caution is in order, however. This site has experienced heavy urbanization during its period of record. These urbanization patterns are likely to have had an impact on the temperature record at "San Francisco," obscuring any background signals of global-scale temperature changes. The influences of urbanization must also be considered at other reliable long-term COOP stations we have identified around the San Francisco metropolitan area (Berkeley, Kentfield, etc.). Some park units in this area, such as PORE and GOGA, incorporate lands that have been more protected from these urbanization influences. Areas such as these could potentially provide more pristine locations to meet the SFAN's objectives of determining the variability and trends in SFAN climate and its impact on biotic and abiotic resources within the network. Unfortunately, as was discussed previously, the long-term stations that were identified at these more pristine locations, such as "Point Reyes Light Stn." And "Mount Tamalpais 2 SW," do not have reliable data.

In addition to defining long-term climate characteristics and trends across the SFAN, and their impacts on SFAN ecosystems, the network is also interested in documenting the characteristics of extreme weather/climate conditions. The significant topographical variations and severe coastal-interior gradients that are present in many SFAN parks means that many of the more extreme characteristics of SFAN climate can only be detected at smaller spatial scales. Very dense weather and climate station coverage would be necessary to sample adequately the local-scale variations in temperature and precipitation that are present in the SFAN, especially near the coast in park units like GOGA and PORE. However, large areas of both parks remain unsampled (e.g., northernmost PORE; coastal sections of PORE along Drakes Bay, Point Lobos in GOGA). Installing new weather stations in areas such as these would be of immediate benefit for SFAN climate monitoring efforts.

Most of the weather and climate stations we identified in PINN are located in the central part of the park unit, concentrated primarily near the east entrance and the Bear Gulch Visitor Center. Much of northern and southern PINN remains unsampled. We acknowledge that these areas within PINN are relatively remote, with no road access points. However, climate monitoring efforts in PINN, particularly those efforts related to better understanding spatial temperature and precipitation variations in the park unit, could benefit greatly by targeting these unsampled areas with new weather stations. Initially, a near-real-time station could be considered for the west entrance or at Chaparral Ranger Station, as the west side of PINN does not appear to be sampled by any weather or climate stations.

5.2. Spatial Variations in Mean Climate

With local variations over short horizontal and vertical distances, topography introduces considerable fine-scale structure to mean climate (temperature and precipitation) within the SFAN park units. Nearer to the coast, severe coast-interior gradients in temperature and precipitation over short distances are also common. Issues encountered in mapping mean climate are discussed in Appendix D and in Redmond et al. (2005).

For areas where new stations will be installed, if only a few new stations will be emplaced, the primary goal should be overall characterization of the main climate elements (temperature and precipitation and their joint relative, snow). This level of characterization generally requires that (a) stations should not be located in deep valley bottoms (cold air drainage pockets) or near excessively steep slopes and (b) stations should be distributed spatially in the major biomes of each park. If such stations already are present in the vicinity, then additional stations would be best used for two important and somewhat competing purposes: (a) add redundancy as backup for loss of data from current stations (or loss of the physical stations) or (b) provide added information on spatial heterogeneity in climate arising from topographic diversity.

5.3. Climate Change Detection

There is much interest in the adaptation of SFAN ecosystems in response to possible future climate change. Potential impacts to sensitive ecosystems, endemic species, and threatened or endangered species are of particular concern. Changes in sea levels and precipitation patterns across the SFAN could cause accelerated shoreline erosion and other problems for coastal environments (NPS 2005). The SFAN region is strongly affected by ENSO cycles. Future climate changes could affect the frequency, intensity, and duration of ENSO events in the area.

The desire for credible, accurate, complete, and long-term climate records—from any location—cannot be overemphasized. Thus, this consideration always should have a high priority. However, because of spatial diversity in climate, monitoring that fills knowledge gaps and provides information on long-term temporal variability in short-distance relationships also will be valuable. We cannot be sure that climate variability and climate change will affect all parts of a given park unit equally. In fact, it is appropriate to speculate that this is not the case, and spatial variations in temporal variability extend to small spatial scales, a consequence of diversity within SFAN in both topography and in land use patterns.

5.4. Aesthetics

This issue arises frequently enough to deserve comment. Standards for quality climate measurements require open exposures away from heat sources, buildings, pavement, close vegetation and tall trees, and human intrusion (thus away from property lines). By their nature, sites that meet these standards are usually quite visible. In many settings (such as heavily forested areas) these sites also are quite rare, making them precisely the same places that managers wish to protect from aesthetic intrusion. The most suitable and scientifically defensible sites frequently are rejected as candidate locations for weather or climate stations. Most stations, therefore, tend to be "hidden" but many of these hidden locations have inferior exposures. Some measure of compromise is nearly always called for in siting weather and climate stations.

The public has vast interest and curiosity in weather and climate, and within the NPS I&M networks, such measurements consistently rate near or at the top of desired public information. There seem to be many possible opportunities for exploiting and embracing this widespread interest within the interpretive mission of the NPS. One way to do this would be to highlight rather than hide these stations and educate the public about the need for adequate siting. A number of weather displays we have encountered during visits have proven inadvertently to serve as counterexamples for how measurements should not be made.

5.5. Information Access

Access to information promotes its use, which in turn promotes attention to station care and maintenance, better data, and more use. An end-to-end view that extends from sensing to decision support is far preferable to isolated and disconnected activities and aids the support infrastructure that is ultimately so necessary for successful, long-term climate monitoring.

Decisions about improvements in monitoring capacity are facilitated greatly by the ability to examine available climate information. Various methods are being created at WRCC to improve access to that information. Web pages providing historic and ongoing climate data, and information from SFAN park units can be accessed at http://www.wrcc.dri.edu/nps. In the event that this URL changes, there still will be links from the main WRCC Web page entitled "Projects" under NPS.

The WRCC has been steadily developing software to summarize data from hourly sites. This has been occurring under the aegis of the RAWS program and a growing array of product generators ranging from daily and monthly data lists to wind roses and hourly frequency distributions. All park data are available to park personnel via an access code (needed only for data listings) that can be acquired by request. The WRCC RAWS Web page is located at http://www.wrcc.dri.edu/wraws or http://www.raws.dri.edu.

Web pages have been developed to provide access not only to historic and ongoing climate data and information from SFAN park units but also to climate-monitoring efforts for SFAN. These pages can be found through http://www.wrcc.dri.edu/nps.

Additional access to more standard climate information is accessible though the previously mentioned Web pages, as well as through http://www.wrcc.dri.edu/summary. These summaries are generally for COOP stations.

5.6. Summarized Conclusions and Recommendations

- SFAN already has plans underway to improve weather and climate station coverage within its park units.
- With the exception of PINN, no SFAN park units have reliable long-term climate records within their boundaries. These park units must support outside sources of long-term climate data.
- Long-term climate records in San Francisco metropolitan area likely are influenced by urbanization effects that obscure background climate variability and change.
- Existing gaps in coverage, particularly in PORE and GOGA, could be addressed in order to improve weather and climate monitoring activities in the SFAN, particularly those activities related to documentating temperature and precipitation variations and extremes in the SFAN
- Most weather and climate stations in PINN are near east entrance or Bear Gulch Visitor Center. Much of northern and southern PINN is unsampled currently. New installations could target these unsampled areas. Initially, PINN could consider installing a new weather station in western PINN, near the west entrance or near Chaparral Ranger Station.

6.0 Literature Cited

American Association of State Climatologists. 1985. Heights and exposure standards for sensors on automated weather stations. The State Climatologist **9**.

Bailey, R. G. 1995. Description of the ecoregions of the United States, 2nd edition. USDA Forest Service, Washington, D.C. Miscellaneous Publication 1391.

Bakun, A. 1990. Global climate change and intensification of coastal ocean upwelling. Science, **247**:198-201.

Barnston, A. G., and R. E. Livezey. 1987. Classification, seasonality and persistence of low-frequency atmospheric circulation patterns. Monthly Weather Review **115**:1083-1126.

Beamish, R. J. and D. R. Bouillon. 1993. Pacific salmon production trends in relation to climate. Canadian Journal of Fisheries and Aquatic Sciences **50**:1002-1016.

Bevis, M., S. Businger, T. A. Herring, C. Rocken, R. A. Anthes, and R. H. Ware. 1992. GPS meteorology: remote sensing of the atmospheric water vapor using the global positioning system. Journal of Geophysical Research **97**:75–94.

Bonan, G. B. 2002. Ecological Climatology: Concepts and Applications. Cambridge University Press.

Bureau of Land Management. 1997. Remote Automatic Weather Station (RAWS) and Remote Environmental Monitoring Systems (REMS) standards. RAWS/REMS Support Facility, Boise, Idaho.

Cayan, D. R., M. D. Dettinger, H. F Diaz, and N. E. Graham. 1998. Decadal variability of precipitation over western North America. Journal of Climate **11**:3148-3166.

Chapin III, F. S., M. S. Torn, and M. Tateno. 1996. Principles of ecosystem sustainability. The American Naturalist **148**:1016-1037.

Croll, D. A., B. B. Marinovic, and M. Mangel. 2000. Climate change and trophic links in coastal upwelling centers. Online. (http://www.ucdavis.edu/publications/annual2000/westgec/Croll/) Accessed 2 July 2003.

Daly, C., R. P. Neilson, and D. L. Phillips. 1994. A statistical-topographic model for mapping climatological precipitation over mountainous terrain. Journal of Applied Meteorology **33**:140-158.

Daly, C., W. P. Gibson, G. H. Taylor, G. L. Johnson, and P. Pasteris. 2002. A knowledge-based approach to the statistical mapping of climate. Climate Research **22**:99-113.

Doggett, M., C. Daly, J. Smith, W. Gibson, G. Taylor, G. Johnson, and P. Pasteris. 2004. High-resolution 1971-2000 mean monthly temperature maps for the western United States. Fourteenth AMS Conf. on Applied Climatology, 84th AMS Annual Meeting. Seattle, Washington, American Meteorological Society, Boston, Massachusetts, January 2004, Paper 4.3, CD-ROM.

Duan, J., M. Bevis, P. Fang, Y. Bock, S. Chiswell, S. Businger, C. Rocken, F. Solheim, T. van Hove, R. Ware, and others. 1996. GPS meteorology: direct estimation of the absolute value of precipitable water. Journal of Applied Meteorology **35**:830-838.

Environmental Protection Agency. 1987. On-site meteorological program guidance for regulatory modeling applications. EPA-450/4-87-013. Environmental Protection Agency, Office of Air Quality Planning and Standards, Research Triangle Park, North Carolina.

Finklin, A. I., and W. C. Fischer. 1990. Weather station handbook –an interagency guide for wildland managers. NFES No. 2140. National Wildfire Coordinating Group, Boise, Idaho.

Gibson, W. P., C. Daly, T. Kittel, D. Nychka, C. Johns, N. Rosenbloom, A. McNab, and G. Taylor. 2002. Development of a 103-year high-resolution climate data set for the conterminous United States. Thirteenth AMS Conf. on Applied Climatology. Portland, Oregon, American Meteorological Society, Boston, MA, May 2002:181-183.

I&M. 2006. I&M Inventories home page. http://science.nature.nps.gov/im/inventory/index.cfm.

Jacobson, M. C., R. J. Charlson, H. Rodhe, and G. H. Orians. 2000. Earth System Science: From Biogeochemical Cycles to Global Change. Academic Press, San Diego.

Karl, T. R., V. E. Derr, D. R. Easterling, C. K. Folland, D. J. Hoffman, S. Levitus, N. Nicholls, D. E. Parker, and G. W. Withee. 1996. Critical issues for long-term climate monitoring. Pages 55-92 *in* T. R. Karl, editor. Long Term Climate Monitoring by the Global Climate Observing System, Kluwer Publishing.

Mantua, N. J. 2000. The Pacific Decadal Oscillation and climate forecasting for North America. Online. (http://www.atmos.washington.edu/~mantua/REPORTS/PDO/PDO_cs.htm) Accessed 27 April 2004.

Mantua, N. J. and S. R. Hare. 2002. The Pacific decadal oscillation. Journal of Oceanography **58**:35-44.

Mock, C. J. 1996. Climatic controls and spatial variations of precipitation in the Western United States. Journal of Climate **9**:1111-1125.

National Assessment Synthesis Team. 2001. Climate Change Impacts on the United States: The Potential Consequences of Climate Variability and Change, Report for the U.S. Global Change Research Program. Cambridge University Press, Cambridge, UK.

National Park Service. 2005. San Francisco Bay Area Network Vital Signs Monitoring Plan. National Park Service. San Francisco Bay Area Network. Golden Gate National Recreation Area. San Francisco, California.

National Research Council. 2001. A Climate Services Vision: First Steps Toward the Future. National Academies Press, Washington, D.C.

National Weather Service. 2003. Forecast Office, San Francisco Bay Area/Monterey, Climatological data. Online. (http://www.wrh.noaa.gov/monterey/climate.html) Accessed 26 June 2003.

National Wildfire Coordinating Group. 2004. National fire danger rating system weather station standards. Report PMS 426.3. National Wildfire Coordinating Group, Boise, Idaho.

Neilson, R. P. 1987. Biotic regionalization and climatic controls in western North America. Vegetatio **70**:135-147.

Oakley, K. L., L. P. Thomas, and S. G. Fancy. 2003. Guidelines for long-term monitoring protocols. Wildlife Society Bulletin **31**:1000-1003.

Redmond, K. T., and R. W. Koch. 1991. Surface climate and streamflow variability in the western United States and their relationship to large-scale circulation indices. Water Resources Research **27**:2381-2399.

Redmond, K. T., D. B. Simeral, and G. D. McCurdy. 2005. Climate monitoring for southwest Alaska national parks: network design and site selection. Report 05-01. Western Regional Climate Center, Reno, Nevada.

Rodriguez-Iturbe, I. 2000. Ecohydrology: A hydrologic perspective of climate-soil-vegetation dynamics. Water Resources Research **36**:3-9.

Schlesinger, W. H. 1997. Biogeochemistry: An Analysis of Global Change. Academic Press, San Diego.

Spellerberg, I. F. 1991. Monitoring Ecological Change. Cambridge University Press.

Tanner, B. D. 1990. Automated weather stations. Remote Sensing Reviews **5**:73-98.

Thurman, H. V. 1988. Introductory Oceanography, 5th edition. Merrill Publishing Company.

Wallace, J. M., and D. S. Gutzler. 1981. Teleconnections in the geopotential height field during the Northern Hemisphere winter. Monthly Weather Review **109**:784-812.

World Meteorological Organization. 1983. Guide to meteorological instruments and methods of observation, No. 8, 5th edition, World Meteorological Organization, Geneva, Switzerland.

World Meteorological Organization. 2005. Organization and planning of intercomparisons of rainfall intensity gauges. World Meteorological Organization, Geneva, Switzerland.

Yuan, L. L., R. A. Anthes, R. H. Ware, C. Rocken, W. D. Bonner, M. G. Bevis, and S. Businger. 1993. Sensing climate change using the global positioning system. Journal of Geophysical Research **98**:14925-14937.

Appendix A. Glossary

Climate—Complete and entire ensemble of statistical descriptors of temporal and spatial properties comprising the behavior of the atmosphere. These descriptors include means, variances, frequency distributions, autocorrelations, spatial correlations and other patterns of association, temporal lags, and element-to-element relationships. The descriptors have a physical basis in flows and reservoirs of energy and mass. Climate and weather phenomena shade gradually into each other and are ultimately inseparable.

Climate Element—(same as Weather Element) Attribute or property of the state of the atmosphere that is measured, estimated, or derived. Examples of climate elements include temperature, wind speed, wind direction, precipitation amount, precipitation type, relative humidity, dewpoint, solar radiation, snow depth, soil temperature at a given depth, etc. A derived element is a function of other elements (like degree days or number of days with rain) and is not measured directly with a sensor. The terms "parameter" or "variable" are not used to describe elements.

Climate Network—Group of climate stations having a common purpose; the group is often owned and maintained by a single organization.

Climate Station—Station where data are collected to track atmospheric conditions over the long-term. Often, this station operates to additional standards to verify long-term consistency. For these stations, the detailed circumstances surrounding a set of measurements (siting and exposure, instrument changes, etc.) are important.

Data—Measurements specifying the state of the physical environment. Does not include metadata.

Data Inventory—Information about overall data properties for each station within a weather or climate network. A data inventory may include start/stop dates, percentages of available data, breakdowns by climate element, counts of actual data values, counts or fractions of data types, etc. These properties must be determined by actually reading the data and thus require the data to be available, accessible, and in a readable format.

NPS I&M Network—A set of NPS park units grouped by a common theme, typically by natural resource and/or geographic region.

Metadata—Information necessary to interpret environmental data properly, organized as a history or series of snapshots—data about data. Examples include details of measurement processes, station circumstances and exposures, assumptions about the site, network purpose and background, types of observations and sensors, pre-treatment of data, access information, maintenance history and protocols, observational methods, archive locations, owner, and station start/end period.

Quality Assurance—Planned and systematic set of activities to provide adequate confidence that products and services are resulting in credible and correct information. Includes quality control.

Quality Control—Evaluation, assessment, and improvement of imperfect data by utilizing other imperfect data.

Station Inventory—Information about a set of stations obtained from metadata that accompany the network or networks. A station inventory can be compiled from direct and indirect reports prepared by others.

Weather—Instantaneous state of the atmosphere at any given time, mainly with respect to its effects on biological activities. As distinguished from climate, weather consists of the short-term (minutes to days) variations in the atmosphere. Popularly, weather is thought of in terms of temperature, precipitation, humidity, wind, sky condition, visibility, and cloud conditions.

Weather Element (same as Climate Element)—Attribute or property of the state of the atmosphere that is measured, estimated, or derived. Examples of weather elements include temperature, wind speed, wind direction, precipitation amount, precipitation type, relative humidity, dewpoint, solar radiation, snow depth, soil temperature at a given depth, etc. A derived weather element is a function of other elements (like degree days or number of days with rain) and is not measured directly. The terms "parameter" and "variable" are not used to describe weather elements.

Weather Network—Group of weather stations usually owned and maintained by a particular organization and usually for a specific purpose.

Weather Station—Station where collected data are intended for near-real-time use with less need for reference to long-term conditions. In many cases, the detailed circumstances of a set of measurements (siting and exposure, instrument changes, etc.) from weather stations are not as important as for climate stations.

Appendix B. Climate-monitoring principles

Since the late 1990s, frequent references have been made to a set of climate-monitoring principles enunciated in 1996 by Tom Karl, director of the NOAA NCDC in Asheville, North Carolina. These monitoring principles also have been referred to informally as the "Ten Commandments of Climate Monitoring." Both versions are given here. In addition, these principles have been adopted by the Global Climate Observing System (GCOS 2004).

(Compiled by Kelly Redmond, Western Regional Climate Center, Desert Research Institute, August 2000.)

B.1. Full Version (Karl et al. 1996)

B.1.1. Effects on climate records of instrument changes, observing practices, observation locations, sampling rates, etc., must be known before such changes are implemented. This can be ascertained through a period where overlapping measurements from old and new observing systems are collected or sometimes by comparing the old and new observing systems with a reference standard. Site stability for in situ measurements, both in terms of physical location and changes in the nearby environment, also should be a key criterion in site selection. Thus, many synoptic network stations, which are primarily used in weather forecasting but also provide valuable climate data, and dedicated climate stations intended to be operational for extended periods must be subject to this policy.

B.1.2. Processing algorithms and changes in these algorithms must be well documented. Documentation should be carried with the data throughout the data-archiving process.

B.1.3. Knowledge of instrument, station, and/or platform history is essential for interpreting and using the data. Changes in instrument sampling time, local environmental conditions for in situ measurements, and other factors pertinent to interpreting the observations and measurements should be recorded as a mandatory part in the observing routine and be archived with the original data.

B.1.4. In situ and other observations with a long, uninterrupted record should be maintained. Every effort should be applied to protect the data sets that have provided long-term, homogeneous observations. "Long-term" for space-based measurements is measured in decades, but for more conventional measurements, "long-term" may be a century or more. Each element in the observational system should develop a list of prioritized sites or observations based on their contribution to long-term climate monitoring.

B.1.5. Calibration, validation, and maintenance facilities are critical requirements for long-term climatic data sets. Homogeneity in the climate record must be assessed routinely, and corrective action must become part of the archived record.

B.1.6. Where feasible, some level of "low-technology" backup to "high-technology" observing systems should be developed to safeguard against unexpected operational failures.

B.1.7. Regions having insufficient data, variables and regions sensitive to change, and key measurements lacking adequate spatial and temporal resolution should be given the highest priority in designing and implementing new climate-observing systems.

B.1.8. Network designers and instrument engineers must receive long-term climate requirements at the outset of the network design process. This is particularly important because most observing systems have been designed for purposes other than long-term climate monitoring. Instruments must possess adequate accuracy with biases small enough to document climate variations and changes.

B.1.9. Much of the development of new observational capabilities and the evidence supporting the value of these observations stem from research-oriented needs or programs. A lack of stable, long-term commitment to these observations and lack of a clear transition plan from research to operations are two frequent limitations in the development of adequate, long-term monitoring capabilities. Difficulties in securing a long-term commitment must be overcome in order to improve the climate-observing system in a timely manner with minimal interruptions.

B.1.10. Data management systems that facilitate access, use, and interpretation are essential. Freedom of access, low cost, mechanisms that facilitate use (directories, catalogs, browse capabilities, availability of metadata on station histories, algorithm accessibility and documentation, etc.) and quality control should guide data management. International cooperation is critical for successful management of data used to monitor long-term climate change and variability.

B.2. Abbreviated version, "Ten Commandments of Climate Monitoring"
B.2.1. Assess the impact of new climate-observing systems or changes to existing systems before they are implemented.

"Thou shalt properly manage network change." (assess effects of proposed changes)

B.2.2. Require a suitable period where measurement from new and old climate-observing systems will overlap.

"Thou shalt conduct parallel testing." (compare old and replacement systems)

B.2.3. Treat calibration, validation, algorithm-change, and data-homogeneity assessments with the same care as the data.

"Thou shalt collect metadata." (fully document system and operating procedures)

B.2.4. Verify capability for routinely assessing the quality and homogeneity of the data including high-resolution data for extreme events.

"Thou shalt assure data quality and continuity." (assess as part of routine operating procedures)

B.2.5. Integrate assessments like those conducted by the International Panel on Climate Change into global climate-observing priorities.

"Thou shalt anticipate the use of data." (integrated environmental assessment; component in operational plan for system)

B.2.6. Maintain long-term weather and climate stations.

"Thou shalt worship historic significance." (maintain homogeneous data sets from long–term, climate-observing systems)

B.2.7. Place high priority on increasing observations in regions lacking sufficient data and in regions sensitive to change and variability.

"Thou shalt acquire complementary data." (new sites to fill observational gaps)

B.2.8. Provide network operators, designers, and instrument engineers with long-term requirements at the outset of the design and implementation phases for new systems.

"Thou shalt specify requirements for climate observation systems." (application and usage of observational data)

B.2.9. Carefully consider the transition from research-observing system to long-term operation.

"Thou shalt have continuity of purpose." (stable long-term commitments)

B.2.10. Focus on data-management systems that facilitate access, use, and interpretation of weather data and metadata.

"Thou shalt provide access to data and metadata." (readily available weather and climate information)

B.3. Literature Cited

Karl, T. R., V. E. Derr, D. R. Easterling, C. K. Folland, D. J. Hoffman, S. Levitus, N. Nicholls, D. E. Parker, and G. W. Withee. 1996. Critical Issues for Long-Term Climate Monitoring. Pages 55-92 *in* T. R. Karl, editor. Long Term Climate Monitoring by the Global Climate Observing System, Kluwer Publishing.

Global Climate Observing System. 2004. Implementation Plan for the Global Observing System for Climate in Support of the UNFCCC. GCOS-92, WMO/TD No. 1219, World Meteorological Organization, Geneva, Switzerland.

Appendix C. Factors in operating a weather/ climate network

C.1. Climate versus Weather

- Climate measurements require _consistency through time._

C.2. Network Purpose

- Anticipated or desired lifetime.
- Breadth of network mission (commitment by needed constituency).
- Dedicated constituency—no network survives without a dedicated constituency.

C.3. Site Identification and Selection

- Spanning gradients in climate or biomes with transects.
- Issues regarding representative spatial scale—site uniformity versus site clustering.
- Alignment with and contribution to network mission.
- Exposure—ability to measure representative quantities.
- Logistics—ability to service station (Always or only in favorable weather?).
- Site redundancy (positive for quality control, negative for extra resources).
- Power—is AC needed?
- Site security—is protection from vandalism needed?
- Permitting often a major impediment and usually underestimated.

C.4. Station Hardware

- Survival—weather is the main cause of lost weather/climate data.
- Robustness of sensors—ability to measure and record in any condition.
- Quality—distrusted records are worthless and a waste of time and money.
  o High quality—will cost up front but pays off later.
  o Low quality—may provide a lower start-up cost but will cost more later (low cost can be expensive).
- Redundancy—backup if sensors malfunction.
- Ice and snow—measurements are much more difficult than rain measurements.
- Severe environments (expense is about two–three times greater than for stations in more benign settings).

C.5. Communications

- Reliability—live data have a much larger constituency.
- One-way or two-way.
  o Retrieval of missed transmissions.
  o Ability to reprogram data logger remotely.
  o Remote troubleshooting abilities.
  o Continuing versus one-time costs.
- Back-up procedures to prevent data loss during communication outages.
- Live communications increase problems but also increase value.

C.6. Maintenance

- Main reason why networks fail (and most networks do eventually fail!).
- <u>Key</u> issue with nearly every network.
- Who will perform maintenance?
- Degree of commitment and motivation to contribute.
- Periodic? On-demand as needed? Preventive?
- Equipment change-out schedules and upgrades for sensors and software.
- Automated stations require <u>skilled</u> and <u>experienced</u> labor.
- Calibration—sensors often drift (climate).
- Site maintenance essential (constant vegetation, surface conditions, nearby influences).
- Typical automated station will cost about $2K per year to maintain.
- Documentation—photos, notes, visits, changes, essential for posterity.
- Planning for equipment life cycle and technological advances.

C.7. Maintaining Programmatic Continuity and Corporate Knowledge

- Long-term vision and commitment needed.
- Institutionalizing versus personalizing—developing appropriate dependencies.

C.8. Data Flow

- Centralized ingest?
- Centralized access to data and data products?
- Local version available?
- Contract out work or do it yourself?
- Quality control of data.
- Archival.
- Metadata—historic information, not a snapshot. Every station should collect metadata.
- Post-collection processing, multiple data-ingestion paths.

C.9. Products

- Most basic product consists of the data values.
- Summaries.
- Write own applications or leverage existing mechanisms?

C.10. Funding

- Prototype approaches as proof of concept.
- Linking and leveraging essential.
- Constituencies—every network <u>needs</u> a constituency.
- Bridging to practical and operational communities? Live data needed.
- Bridging to counterpart research efforts and initiatives—funding source.
- Creativity, resourcefulness, and persistence usually are essential to success.

C.11. Final Comments

- Deployment is by far the easiest part in operating a network.
- Maintenance is the main issue.
- Best analogy: Operating a network is like raising a child; it requires constant attention.

Source: Western Regional Climate Center (WRCC)

Appendix D. General design considerations for weather/climate-monitoring programs

The process for designing a climate-monitoring program benefits from anticipating design and protocol issues discussed here. Much of this material is been excerpted from a report addressing the Channel Islands National Park (Redmond and McCurdy 2005), where an example is found illustrating how these factors can be applied to a specific setting. Many national park units possess some climate or meteorology feature that sets them apart from more familiar or "standard" settings.

D.1. Introduction

There are several criteria that must be used in deciding to deploy new stations and where these new stations should be sited.

- Where are existing stations located?
- Where have data been gathered in the past (discontinued locations)?
- Where would a new station fill a knowledge gap about basic, long-term climatic averages for an area of interest?
- Where would a new station fill a knowledge gap about how climate behaves over time?
- As a special case for behavior over time, what locations might be expected to show a more sensitive response to climate change?
- How do answers to the preceding questions depend on the climate element? Are answers the same for precipitation, temperature, wind, snowfall, humidity, etc.?
- What role should manual measurements play? How should manual measurements interface with automated measurements?
- Are there special technical or management issues, either present or anticipated in the next 5–15 years, requiring added climate information?
- What unique information is provided in addition to information from existing sites? "Redundancy is bad."
- What nearby information is available to estimate missing observations because observing systems always experience gaps and lose data? "Redundancy is good."
- How would logistics and maintenance affect these decisions?

In relation to the preceding questions, there are several topics that should be considered. The following topics are not listed in a particular order.

D.1.1. Network Purpose

Humans seem to have an almost reflexive need to measure temperature and precipitation, along with other climate elements. These reasons span a broad range from utilitarian to curiosity-driven. Although there are well-known recurrent patterns of need and data use, new uses are always appearing. The number of uses ranges in the thousands. Attempts have been made to categorize such uses (see NRC 1998; 2001). Because climate measurements are accumulated over a long time, they should be treated as multi-purpose and should be undertaken in a manner that serves the widest possible applications. Some applications remain constant, while others rise and fall in importance. An insistent issue today may subside, while the next pressing issue of tomorrow barely may be anticipated. The notion that humans might affect the climate of the entire Earth was nearly unimaginable when the national USDA (later NOAA) cooperative weather network began in the late 1800s. Abundant experience has shown, however, that there always will be a demand for a history record of climate measurements and their properties. Experience also shows that there is an expectation that climate measurements will be taken and made available to the general public.

An exhaustive list of uses for data would fill many pages and still be incomplete. In broad terms, however, there are needs to document environmental conditions that disrupt or otherwise affect park operations (e.g., storms and droughts). Design and construction standards are determined by climatological event frequencies that exceed certain thresholds. Climate is a determinant that sometimes attracts and sometimes discourages visitors. Climate may play a large part in the park experience (e.g., Death Valley and heat are nearly synonymous). Some park units are large enough to encompass spatial or elevation diversity in climate and the sequence of events can vary considerably inside or close to park boundaries. That is, temporal trends and statistics may not be the same everywhere, and this spatial structure should be sampled. The granularity of this structure depends on the presence of topography or large climate gradients or both, such as that found along the U.S. West Coast in summer with the rapid transition from the marine layer to the hot interior.

Plant and animal communities and entire ecosystems react to every nuance in the physical environment. No aspect of weather and climate goes undetected in the natural world. Wilson (1998) proposed "an informal rule of biological evolution" that applies here: "If an organic sensor can be imagined that is capable of detecting any particular environmental signal, a species exists somewhere that possesses this sensor." Every weather and climate event, whether dull or extraordinary to humans, matters to some organism. Dramatic events and creeping incremental change both have consequences to living systems. Extreme events or disturbances can "reset the clock" or "shake up the system" and lead to reverberations that last for years to centuries or longer. Slow change can carry complex nonlinear systems (e.g., any living assemblage) into states where chaotic transitions and new behavior occur. These changes are seldom predictable, typically are observed after the fact, and understood only in retrospect. Climate changes may not be exciting, but as a well-known atmospheric scientist, Mike Wallace, from the University of Washington once noted, "subtle does not mean unimportant."

Thus, individuals who observe the climate should be able to record observations accurately and depict both rapid and slow changes. In particular, an array of artificial influences easily can confound detection of slow changes. The record as provided can contain both real climate variability (that took place in the atmosphere) and fake climate variability (that arose directly from the way atmospheric changes were observed and recorded). As an example, trees growing near a climate station with an excellent anemometer will make it appear that the wind gradually slowed down over many years. Great care must be taken to protect against sources of fake climate variability on the longer-time scales of years to decades. Processes leading to the observed climate are not stationary; rather these processes draw from probability distributions that vary with time. For this reason, climatic time series do not exhibit statistical stationarity. The implications are manifold. There are no true climatic "normals" to which climate inevitably must return. Rather, there are broad ranges of climatic conditions. Climate does not demonstrate exact repetition but instead continual fluctuation and sometimes approximate repetition. In addition, there is always new behavior waiting to occur. Consequently, the business of climate monitoring is never finished, and there is no point where we can state confidently that "enough" is known.

D.1.2. Robustness
The most frequent cause for loss of weather data is the weather itself, the very thing we wish to record. The design of climate and weather observing programs should consider the meteorological equivalent of "peaking power" employed by utilities. Because environmental disturbances have significant effects on ecologic systems, sensors, data loggers, and communications networks should be able to function during the most severe conditions that realistically can be anticipated over the next 50–100 years. Systems designed in this manner are less likely to fail under more ordinary conditions, as well as more likely to transmit continuous, quality data for both tranquil and active periods.

D.1.3. Weather versus Climate
For "weather" measurements, pertaining to what is approximately happening here and now, small moves and changes in exposure are not as critical. For "climate" measurements, where values from different points in time are compared, siting and exposure are critical factors, and it is vitally important that the observing circumstances remain essentially unchanged over the duration of the station record.

Station moves can affect different elements to differing degrees. Even small moves of several meters, especially vertically, can affect temperature records. Hills and knolls act differently from the bottoms of small swales, pockets, or drainage channels (Whiteman 2000; Geiger et al. 2003). Precipitation is probably less subject to change with moves of 50–100 m than other elements (that is, precipitation has less intrinsic variation in small spaces) except if wind flow over the gauge is affected.

D.1.4. Physical Setting
Siting and exposure, and their continuity and consistency through time, significantly influence the climate records produced by a station. These two terms have overlapping connotations. We use the term "siting" in a more general sense, reserving the term "exposure" generally for the particular circumstances affecting the ability of an instrument to record measurements that are representative of the desired spatial or temporal scale.

D.1.5. Measurement Intervals
Climatic processes occur continuously in time, but our measurement systems usually record in discrete chunks of time: for example, seconds, hours, or days. These measurements often are referred to as "systematic" measurements. Interval averages may hide active or interesting periods of highly intense activity. Alternatively, some systems record "events" when a certain threshold of activity is exceeded (examples: another millimeter of precipitation has fallen, another kilometer of wind has moved past, the temperature has changed by a degree, a gust higher than 9.9 m/s has been measured). When this occurs, measurements from all sensors are reported. These measurements are known as "breakpoint" data. In relatively unchanging conditions (long calm periods or rainless weeks, for example), event recorders should send a signal that they are still "alive and well." If systematic recorders are programmed to note and periodically report the highest, lowest, and mean value within each time interval, the likelihood

is reduced that interesting behavior will be glossed over or lost. With the capacity of modern data loggers, it is recommended to record and report extremes within the basic time increment (e.g., hourly or 10 minutes). This approach also assists quality-control procedures.

There is usually a trade-off between data volume and time increment, and most automated systems now are set to record approximately hourly. A number of field stations maintained by WRCC are programmed to record in 5- or 10-minute increments, which readily serve to construct an hourly value. However, this approach produces 6–12 times as much data as hourly data. These systems typically do not record details of events at sub-interval time scales, but they easily can record peak values, or counts of threshold exceedance, within the time intervals.

Thus, for each time interval at an automated station, we recommend that several kinds of information—mean or sum, extreme maximum and minimum, and sometimes standard deviation—be recorded. These measurements are useful for quality control and other purposes. Modern data loggers and office computers have quite high capacity. Diagnostic information indicating the state of solar chargers or battery voltages and their extremes is of great value. This topic will be discussed in greater detail in a succeeding section.

Automation also has made possible adaptive or intelligent monitoring techniques where systems vary the recording rate based on detection of the behavior of interest by the software. Sub-interval behavior of interest can be masked on occasion (e.g., a 5-minute extreme downpour with high-erosive capability hidden by an innocuous hourly total). Most users prefer measurements that are systematic in time because they are much easier to summarize and manipulate.

For breakpoint data produced by event reporters, there also is a need to send periodically a signal that the station is still functioning, even though there is nothing more to report. "No report" does not necessarily mean "no data," and it is important to distinguish between the actual observation that was recorded and the content of that observation (e.g., an observation of "0.00" is not the same as "no observation").

D.1.6. Mixed Time Scales
There are times when we may wish to combine information from radically different scales. For example, over the past 100 years we may want to know how the frequency of 5-minute precipitation peaks has varied or how the frequency of peak 1-second wind gusts have varied. We may also want to know over this time if nearby vegetation gradually has grown up to increasingly block the wind or to slowly improve precipitation catch. Answers to these questions require knowledge over a wide range of time scales.

D.1.7. Elements
For manual measurements, the typical elements recorded included temperature extremes, precipitation, and snowfall/snow depth. Automated measurements typically include temperature, precipitation, humidity, wind speed and direction, and solar radiation. An exception to this exists in very windy locations where precipitation is difficult to measure accurately. Automated measurements of snow are improving, but manual measurements are still preferable, as long as shielding is present. Automated measurement of frozen precipitation presents numerous challenges that have not been resolved fully, and the best gauges are quite expensive ($3–8K).

Soil temperatures also are included sometimes. Soil moisture is extremely useful, but measurements are not made at many sites. In addition, care must be taken in the installation and maintenance of instruments used in measuring soil moisture. Soil properties vary tremendously in short distances as well, and it is often very difficult ("impossible") to accurately document these variations (without digging up all the soil!). In cooler climates, ultrasonic sensors that detect snow depth are becoming commonplace.

D.1.8. Wind Standards

Wind varies the most in the shortest distance, since it always decreases to zero near the ground and increases rapidly (approximately logarithmically) with height near the ground. Changes in anemometer height obviously will affect distribution of wind speed as will changes in vegetation, obstructions such as buildings, etc. A site that has a 3-m (10-ft) mast clearly will be less windy than a site that has a 6-m (20-ft) or 10-m (33-ft) mast. Historically, many U.S. airports (FAA and NWS) and most current RAWS sites have used a standard 6-m (20-ft) mast for wind measurements. Some NPS RAWS sites utilize shorter masts. Over the last decade, as Automated Surface Observing Systems (ASOSs, mostly NWS) and Automated Weather Observing Systems (AWOSs, mostly FAA) have been deployed at most airports, wind masts have been raised to 8 or 10 m (26 or 33 ft), depending on airplane clearance. The World Meteorological Organization recommends 10 m as the height for wind measurements (WMO 1983; 2005), and more groups are migrating slowly to this standard. The American Association of State Climatologists (AASC 1985) have recommended that wind be measured at 3 m, a standard geared more for agricultural applications than for general purpose uses where higher levels usually are preferred. Different anemometers have different starting thresholds; therefore, areas that frequently experience very light winds may not produce wind measurements thus affecting long-term mean estimates of wind speed. For both sustained winds (averages over a short interval of 2–60 minutes) and especially for gusts, the duration of the sampling interval makes a considerable difference. For the same wind history, 1–second gusts are higher than gusts averaging 3 seconds, which in turn are greater than 5-second averages, so that the same sequence would be described with different numbers (all three systems and more are in use). Changes in the averaging procedure, or in height or exposure, can lead to "false" or "fake" climate change with no change in actual climate. Changes in any of these should be noted in the metadata.

D.1.9. Wind Nomenclature

Wind is a vector quantity having a direction and a speed. Directions can be two- or three-dimensional; they will be three-dimensional if the vertical component is important. In all common uses, winds always are denoted by the direction they blow *from* (north wind or southerly breeze). This convention exists because wind often brings weather, and thus our attention is focused upstream. However, this approach contrasts with the way ocean currents are viewed. Ocean currents usually are denoted by the direction they are moving *towards* (eastward current moves from west to east). In specialized applications (such as in atmospheric modeling), wind velocity vectors point in the direction that the wind is blowing. Thus, a southwesterly wind (from the southwest) has both northward and eastward (to the north and to the east) components. Except near mountains, wind cannot blow up or down near the ground, so the vertical component of wind often is approximated as zero, and the horizontal component is emphasized.

D.1.10. Frozen Precipitation

Frozen precipitation is more difficult to measure than liquid precipitation, especially with automated techniques. Sevruk and Harmon (1984), Goodison et al. (1998), and Yang et al. (1998; 2001) provide many of the reasons to explain this. The importance of frozen precipitation varies greatly from one setting to another. This subject was discussed in greater detail in a related inventory and monitoring report for the Alaska park units (Redmond et al. 2005).

In climates that receive frozen precipitation, a decision must be made whether or not to try to record such events accurately. This usually means that the precipitation must be turned into liquid either by falling into an antifreeze fluid solution that is then weighed or by heating the precipitation enough to melt and fall through a measuring mechanism such as a nearly-balanced tipping bucket. Accurate measurements from the first approach require expensive gauges; tipping buckets can achieve this resolution readily but are more apt to lose some or all precipitation. Improvements have been made to the heating mechanism on the NWS tipping-bucket gauge used for the ASOS to correct its numerous deficiencies making it less problematic; however, this gauge is not inexpensive. A heat supply needed to melt frozen precipitation usually requires more energy than renewable energy (solar panels or wind recharging) can provide thus AC power is needed. Periods of frozen precipitation or rime often provide less-than-optimal recharging conditions with heavy clouds, short days, low-solar-elevation angles and more horizon blocking, and cold temperatures causing additional drain on the battery.

D.1.11. Save or Lose

A second consideration with precipitation is determining if the measurement should be saved (as in weighing systems) or lost (as in tipping-bucket systems). With tipping buckets, after the water has passed through the tipping mechanism, it usually just drops to the ground. Thus, there is no checksum to ensure that the sum of all the tips adds up to what has been saved in a reservoir at some location. By contrast, the weighing gauges continually accumulate until the reservoir is emptied, the reported value is the total reservoir content (for example, the height of the liquid column in a tube), and the incremental precipitation is the difference in depth between two known times. These weighing gauges do not always have the same fine resolution. Some gauges only record to the nearest centimeter, which is usually acceptable for hydrology but not necessarily for other needs. (For reference, a millimeter of precipitation can get a person in street clothes quite wet.) Other weighing gauges are capable of measuring to the 0.25-mm (0.01-in.) resolution but do not have as much capacity and must be emptied more often. Day/night and storm-related thermal expansion and contraction and sometimes wind shaking can cause fluid pressure from accumulated totals to go up and down in SNOTEL gauges by small increments (commonly 0.3-3 cm, or 0.01–0.10 ft) leading to "negative precipitation" followed by similarly non-real light precipitation when, in fact, no change took place in the amount of accumulated precipitation.

D.1.12. Time

Time should always be in local standard time (LST), and daylight savings time (DST) should never be used under any circumstances with automated equipment and timers. Using DST leads to one duplicate hour, one missing hour, and a season of displaced values, as well as needless confusion and a data-management nightmare. Absolute time, such as Greenwich Mean Time (GMT) or Coordinated Universal Time (UTC), also can be used because these formats are unambiguously translatable. Since measurements only provide information about what already *has* occurred or *is* occurring and not what *will* occur, they should always be assigned to the *ending time* of the associated interval with hour 24 marking the end of the last hour of the day. In this system, midnight always represents the end of the day, not the start. To demonstrate the importance of this differentiation, we have encountered situations where police officers seeking corroborating weather data could not recall whether the time on their crime report from a year ago was the starting midnight or the ending midnight! Station positions should be known to within a few meters, easily accomplished with GPS, so that time zones and solar angles can be determined accurately.

D.1.13. Automated versus Manual

Most of this report has addressed automated measurements. Historically, most measurements are manual and typically collected once a day. In many cases, manual measurements continue because of habit, usefulness, and desire for continuity over time. Manual measurements are extremely useful and when possible should be encouraged. However, automated measurements are becoming more common. For either, it is important to record time in a logically consistent manner.

It should not be automatically assumed that newer data and measurements are "better" than older data or that manual data are "worse" than automated data. Older or simpler manual measurements are often of very high quality even if they sometimes are not in the most convenient digital format.

There is widespread desire to use automated systems to reduce human involvement. This is admirable and understandable, but every automated weather/climate station or network requires significant human attention and maintenance. A telling example concerns the Oklahoma Mesonet (see Brock et al. 1995, and bibliography at http://www.mesonet.ou.edu), a network of about 115 high–quality, automated meteorological stations spread over Oklahoma, where about 80 percent of the annual ($2–3M) budget is nonetheless allocated to humans with only about 20 percent allocated to equipment.

D.1.14. Manual Conventions

Manual measurements typically are made once a day. Elements usually consist of maximum and minimum temperature, temperature at observation time, precipitation, snowfall, snow depth, and sometimes evaporation, wind, or other information. Since it is not actually known when extremes occurred, the only logical approach, and the nationwide convention, is to ascribe the entire measurement to the time-interval date and to enter it on the form in that way. For morning observers (for example, 8 am to 8 am), this means that the maximum temperature written for today often is from yesterday afternoon and sometimes the minimum temperature for the 24-hr period actually occurred yesterday morning. However, this is understood and expected. It is often a surprise to observers to see how many maximum temperatures do not occur in the afternoon and how many minimum temperatures do not occur in the predawn hours. This is especially true in environments that are colder, higher, northerly, cloudy, mountainous, or coastal. As long as this convention is strictly followed every day, it has been shown that truly excellent climate records can result (Redmond 1992). Manual observers should reset equipment only one time per day at the official observing time. Making more than one measurement a day is discouraged strongly; this practice results in a hybrid record that is too difficult to interpret. The only exception is for total daily snowfall. New snowfall can be measured up to four times per day with no observations closer than six hours. It is well known that more frequent measurement of snow increases the annual total because compaction is a continuous process.

Two main purposes for climate observations are to establish the long-term averages for given locations and to track variations in climate. Broadly speaking, these purposes address topics of absolute and relative climate behavior. Once absolute behavior has been "established" (a task that is never finished because long-term averages continue to vary in time)—temporal variability quickly becomes the item of most interest.

D.2. Representativeness

Having discussed important factors to consider when new sites are installed, we now turn our attention to site "representativeness." In popular usage, we often encounter the notion that a site is "representative" of another site if it receives the same annual precipitation or records the same annual temperature or if some other element-specific, long-term average has a similar value. This notion of representativeness has a certain limited validity, but there are other aspects of this idea that need to be considered.

A climate monitoring site also can be said to be representative if climate records from that site show sufficiently strong temporal correlations with a large number of locations over a sufficiently large area. If station A receives 20 cm a year and station B receives 200 cm a year, these climates obviously receive quite differing amounts of precipitation. However, if their monthly, seasonal, or annual correlations are high (for example, 0.80 or higher for a particular time scale), one site can be used as a surrogate for estimating values at the other if measurements for a particular month, season, or year are missing. That is, a wet or dry month at one station is also a wet or dry month (relative to its own mean) at the comparison station. Note that high correlations on one time scale do not imply automatically that high correlations will occur on other time scales.

Likewise, two stations having similar mean climates (for example, similar annual precipitation) might not co-vary in close synchrony (for example, coastal versus interior). This may be considered a matter of climate "affiliation" for a particular location.

Thus, the representativeness of a site can refer either to the basic climatic averages for a given duration (or time window within the annual cycle) or to the extent that the site co-varies in time with respect to all surrounding locations. One site can be representative of another in the first sense but not the second, or vice versa, or neither, or both—all combinations are possible.

If two sites are perfectly correlated then, in a sense, they are "redundant." However, redundancy has value because all sites will experience missing data especially with automated equipment in rugged environments and harsh climates where outages and other problems nearly can be guaranteed. In many cases, those outages are caused by the weather, particularly by unusual weather and the very conditions we most wish to know about. Methods for filling in those values will require proxy information from this or other nearby networks. Thus, redundancy is a virtue rather than a vice.

In general, the cooperative stations managed by the NWS have produced much longer records than automated stations like RAWS or SNOTEL stations. The RAWS stations often have problems with precipitation, especially in winter, or with missing data, so that low correlations may be data problems rather than climatic dissimilarity. The RAWS records also are relatively short, so correlations should be interpreted with care. In performing and interpreting such analyses, however, we must remember that there are physical climate reasons and observational reasons why stations within a short distance (even a few tens or hundreds of meters) may not correlate well.

D.2.1. Temporal Behavior

It is possible that high correlations will occur between station pairs during certain portions of the year (i.e., January) but low correlations may occur during other portions of the year (e.g., September or October). The relative contributions of these seasons to the annual total (for precipitation) or average (for temperature) and the correlations for each month are both factors in the correlation of an aggregated time window of longer duration that encompasses those seasons (e.g., one of the year definitions such as calendar year or water year). A complete and careful evaluation ideally would include such a correlation analysis but requires more resources and data. Note that it also is possible and frequently is observed that temperatures are highly correlated while precipitation is not or vice versa, and these relations can change according to the time of year. If two stations are well correlated for all climate elements for all portions of the year, then they can be considered redundant.

With scarce resources, the initial strategy should be to try to identify locations that do not correlate particularly well, so that each new site measures something new that cannot be guessed easily from the behavior of surrounding sites. (An important caveat here is that lack of such correlation could be a result of physical climate behavior and not a result of faults with the actual measuring process; i.e., by unrepresentative or simply poor-quality data. Unfortunately, we seldom have perfect climate data.) As additional sites are added, we usually wish for some combination of unique and redundant sites to meet what amounts to essentially orthogonal constraints: new information and more reliably-furnished information.

A common consideration is whether to observe on a ridge or in a valley, given the resources to place a single station within a particular area of a few square kilometers. Ridge and valley stations will correlate very well for temperatures when lapse conditions prevail, particularly summer daytime temperatures. In summer at night or winter at daylight, the picture will be more mixed and correlations will be lower. In winter at night when inversions are common and even the rule, correlations may be zero or even negative and perhaps even more divergent as the two sites are on opposite sides of the inversion. If we had the luxury of locating stations everywhere, we would find that ridge tops generally correlate very well with other ridge tops and similarly valleys with other valleys, but ridge tops correlate well with valleys only under certain circumstances. Beyond this, valleys and ridges having similar orientations usually will correlate better with each other than those with perpendicular orientations, depending on their orientation with respect to large-scale wind flow and solar angles.

Unfortunately, we do not have stations everywhere, so we are forced to use the few comparisons that we have and include a large dose of intelligent reasoning, using what we have observed elsewhere. In performing and interpreting such analyses, we must remember that there are physical climatic reasons and observational reasons why stations within a short distance (even a few tens or hundreds of meters) may not correlate well.

Examples of correlation analyses include those for the Channel Islands and for southwest Alaska, which can be found in Redmond and McCurdy (2005) and Redmond et al. (2005). These examples illustrate what can be learned from correlation analyses. Spatial correlations generally vary by time of year. Thus, results should be displayed in the form of annual correlation cycles— for monthly mean temperature and monthly total precipitation and perhaps other climate elements like wind or humidity—between station pairs selected for climatic setting and data availability and quality.

In general, the COOP stations managed by the NWS have produced much longer records than have automated stations like RAWS or SNOTEL stations. The RAWS stations also often have problems with precipitation, especially in winter or with missing data, so that low correlations may be data problems rather than climate dissimilarity. The RAWS records are much shorter, so correlations should be interpreted with care, but these stations are more likely to be in places of interest for remote or under-sampled regions.

D.2.2. Spatial Behavior

A number of techniques exist to interpolate from isolated point values to a spatial domain. For example, a common technique is simple inverse distance weighting. Critical to the success of the simplest of such techniques is that some other property of the spatial domain, one that is influential for the mapped element, does not vary significantly. Topography greatly influences precipitation, temperature, wind, humidity, and most other meteorological elements. Thus, this criterion clearly is not met in any region having extreme topographic diversity. In such circumstances, simple Cartesian distance may have little to do with how rapidly correlation deteriorates from one site to the next, and in fact, the correlations can decrease readily from a mountain to a valley and then increase again on the next mountain. Such structure in the fields of spatial correlation is not seen in the relatively (statistically) well-behaved flat areas like those in the eastern U.S.

To account for dominating effects such as topography and inland–coastal differences that exist in certain regions, some kind of additional knowledge must be brought to bear to produce meaningful, physically plausible, and observationally based interpolations. Historically, this has proven to be an extremely difficult problem, especially to perform objective and repeatable analyses. An analysis performed for southwest Alaska (Redmond et al. 2005) concluded that the PRISM (Parameter Regression on Independent Slopes Model) maps (Daly et al. 1994; 2002; Gibson et al. 2002; Doggett et al. 2004) were probably the best available. An analysis by Simpson et al. (2005) further discussed many issues in the mapping of Alaska's climate and resulted in the same conclusion about PRISM.

D.2.3. Climate-Change Detection

Although general purpose climate stations should be situated to address all aspects of climate variability, it is desirable that they also be in locations that are more sensitive to climate change from natural or anthropogenic influences should it begin to occur. The question here is how well we know such sensitivities. The climate-change issue is quite complex because it encompasses more than just greenhouse gasses.

Sites that are in locations or climates particularly vulnerable to climate change should be favored. How this vulnerability is determined is a considerably challenging research issue. Candidate locations or situations are those that lie on the border between two major biomes or just inside the edge of one or the other. In these cases, a slight movement of the boundary in anticipated direction (toward "warmer," for example) would be much easier to detect as the boundary moves past the site and a different set of biota begin to be established. Such a vegetative or ecologic response would be more visible and would take less time to establish as a real change than would a smaller change in the center of the distribution range of a marker or key species.

D.2.4. Element-Specific Differences
The various climate elements (temperature, precipitation, cloudiness, snowfall, humidity, wind speed and direction, solar radiation) do not vary through time in the same sequence or manner nor should they necessarily be expected to vary in this manner. The spatial patterns of variability should not be expected to be the same for all elements. These patterns also should not be expected to be similar for all months or seasons. The suitability of individual sites for measurement also varies from one element to another. A site that has a favorable exposure for temperature or wind may not have a favorable exposure for precipitation or snowfall. A site that experiences proper air movement may be situated in a topographic channel, such as a river valley or a pass, which restricts the range of wind directions and affects the distribution of speed-direction categories.

D.2.5. Logistics and Practical Factors
Even with the most advanced scientific rationale, sites in some remote or climatically challenging settings may not be suitable because of the difficulty in servicing and maintaining equipment. Contributing to these challenges are scheduling difficulties, animal behavior, snow burial, icing, snow behavior, access and logistical problems, and the weather itself. Remote and elevated sites usually require far more attention and expense than a rain-dominated, easily accessible valley location.

For climate purposes, station exposure and the local environment should be maintained in their original state (vegetation especially), so that changes seen are the result of regional climate variations and not of trees growing up, bushes crowding a site, surface albedo changing, fire clearing, etc. Repeat photography has shown many examples of slow environmental change in the vicinity of a station in rather short time frames (5–20 years), and this technique should be employed routinely and frequently at all locations. In the end, logistics, maintenance, and other practical factors almost always determine the success of weather- and climate-monitoring activities.

D.2.6. Personnel Factors
Many past experiences (almost exclusively negative) strongly support the necessity to place primary responsibility for station deployment and maintenance in the hands of seasoned, highly qualified, trained, and meticulously careful personnel, the more experienced the better. Over

time, even in "benign" climates but especially where harsher conditions prevail, every conceivable problem will occur and both the usual and unusual should be anticipated: weather, animals, plants, salt, sensor and communication failure, windblown debris, corrosion, power failures, vibrations, avalanches, snow loading and creep, corruption of the data logger program, etc. An ability to anticipate and forestall such problems, a knack for innovation and improvisation, knowledge of electronics, practical and organizational skills, and presence of mind to bring the various small but vital parts, spares, tools, and diagnostic troubleshooting equipment are highly valued qualities. Especially when logistics are so expensive, a premium should be placed on using experienced personnel, since the slightest and seemingly most minor mistake can render a station useless or, even worse, uncertain. Exclusive reliance on individuals without this background can be costly and almost always will result eventually in unnecessary loss of data. Skilled labor and an apprenticeship system to develop new skilled labor will greatly reduce (but not eliminate) the types of problems that can occur in operating a climate network.

D.3. Site Selection
In addition to considerations identified previously in this appendix, various factors need to be considered in selecting sites for new or augmented instrumentation.

D.3.1. Equipment and Exposure Factors
D.3.1.1. Measurement Suite: All sites should measure temperature, humidity, wind, solar radiation, and snow depth. Precipitation measurements are more difficult but probably should be attempted with the understanding that winter measurements may be of limited or no value unless an all-weather gauge has been installed. Even if an all-weather gauge has been installed, it is desirable to have a second gauge present that operates on a different principle—for example, a fluid-based system like those used in the SNOTEL stations in tandem with a higher–resolution, tipping bucket gauge for summertime. Without heating, a tipping bucket gauge usually is of use only when temperatures are above freezing and when temperatures have not been below freezing for some time, so that accumulated ice and snow is not melting and being recorded as present precipitation. Gauge undercatch is a significant issue in snowy climates, so shielding should be considered for all gauges designed to work over the winter months. It is very important to note the presence or absence of shielding, the type of shielding, and the dates of installation or removal of the shielding.

D.3.1.2. Overall Exposure: The ideal, general all-purpose site has gentle slopes, is open to the sun and the wind, has a natural vegetative cover, avoids strong local (less than 200 m) influences, and represents a reasonable compromise among all climate elements. The best temperature sites are not the best precipitation sites, and the same is true for other elements. Steep topography in the immediate vicinity should be avoided unless settings where precipitation is affected by steep topography are being deliberately sought or a mountaintop or ridgeline is the desired location. The potential for disturbance should be considered: fire and flood risk, earth movement, wind-borne debris, volcanic deposits or lahars, vandalism, animal tampering, and general human encroachment are all factors.

D.3.1.3. Elevation: Mountain climates do not vary in time in exactly the same manner as adjoining valley climates. This concept is emphasized when temperature inversions are present to a greater degree and during precipitation when winds rise up the slopes at the same angle.

There is considerable concern that mountain climates will be (or already are) changing and perhaps changing differently than lowland climates, which has direct and indirect consequences for plant and animal life in the more extreme zones. Elevations of special significance are those that are near the mean rain/snow line for winter, near the tree line, and near the mean annual freezing level (all of these may not be quite the same). Because the lapse rates in wet climates often are nearly moist-adiabatic during the main precipitation seasons, measurements at one elevation may be extrapolated to nearby elevations. In drier climates and in the winter, temperature and to a lesser extent wind will show various elevation profiles.

D.3.1.4. Transects: The concept of observing transects that span climatic gradients is sound. This is not always straightforward in topographically uneven terrain, but these transects could still be arranged by setting up station(s) along the coast; in or near passes atop the main coastal interior drainage divide; and inland at one, two, or three distances into the interior lowlands. Transects need not—and by dint of topographic constraints probably cannot—be straight lines, but the closer that a line can be approximated the better. The main point is to systematically sample the key points of a behavioral transition without deviating too radically from linearity.

D.3.1.5. Other Topographic Considerations: There are various considerations with respect to local topography. Local topography can influence wind (channeling, upslope/downslope, etc.), precipitation (orographic enhancement, downslope evaporation, catch efficiency, etc.), and temperature (frost pockets, hilltops, aspect, mixing or decoupling from the overlying atmosphere, bowls, radiative effects, etc.), to different degrees at differing scales. In general, for measurements to be areally representative, it is better to avoid these local effects to the extent that they can be identified before station deployment (once deployed, it is desirable not to move a station). The primary purpose of a climate-monitoring network should be to serve as an infrastructure in the form of a set of benchmark stations for comparing other stations. Sometimes, however, it is exactly these local phenomena that we want to capture. Living organisms, especially plants, are affected by their immediate environment, whether it is representative of a larger setting or not. Specific measurements of limited scope and duration made for these purposes then can be tied to the main benchmarks. This experience is useful also in determining the complexity needed in the benchmark monitoring process in order to capture particular phenomena at particular space and time scales.

Sites that drain (cold air) well generally are better than sites that allow cold air to pool. Slightly sloped areas (1 degree is fine) or small benches from tens to hundreds of meters above streams are often favorable locations. Furthermore, these sites often tend to be out of the path of hazards (like floods) and to have rocky outcroppings where controlling vegetation will not be a major concern. Benches or wide spots on the rise between two forks of a river system are often the only flat areas and sometimes jut out to give greater exposure to winds from more directions.

D.3.1.6. Prior History: The starting point in designing a program is to determine what kinds of observations have been collected over time, by whom, in what manner, and if these observation are continuing to the present time. It also may be of value to "re-occupy" the former site of a station that is now inactive to provide some measure of continuity or a reference point from the past. This can be of value even if continuous observations were not made during the entire intervening period.

D.3.2. Element-Specific Factors

D.3.2.1. Temperature: An open exposure with uninhibited air movement is the preferred setting. The most common measurement is made at approximately eye level, 1.5–2.0 m. In snowy locations sensors should be at least one meter higher than the deepest snowpack expected in the next 50 years or perhaps 2–3 times the depth of the average maximum annual depth. Sensors should be shielded above and below from solar radiation (bouncing off snow), from sunrise/sunset horizontal input, and from vertical rock faces. Sensors should be clamped tightly, so that they do not swivel away from level stacks of radiation plates. Nearby vegetation should be kept away from the sensors (several meters). Growing vegetation should be cut to original conditions. Small hollows and swales can cool tremendously at night, and it is best avoid these areas. Side slopes of perhaps a degree or two of angle facilitate air movement and drainage and, in effect, sample a large area during nighttime hours. The very bottom of a valley should be avoided. Temperature can change substantially from moves of only a few meters. Situations have been observed where flat and seemingly uniform conditions (like airport runways) appear to demonstrate different climate behaviors over short distances of a few tens or hundreds of meters (differences of 5–10°C). When snow is on the ground, these microclimatic differences can be stronger, and differences of 2–5°C can occur in the short distance between the thermometer and the snow surface on calm evenings.

D.3.2.2. Precipitation (liquid): Calm locations with vegetative or artificial shielding are preferred. Wind will adversely impact readings; therefore, the less the better. Wind effects on precipitation are far less for rain than for snow. Devices that "save" precipitation present advantages, but most gauges are built to dump precipitation as it falls or to empty periodically. Automated gauges give both the amount and the timing. Simple backups that record only the total precipitation since the last visit have a certain advantage (for example, storage gauges or lengths of PVC pipe perhaps with bladders on the bottom). The following question should be asked: Does the total precipitation from an automated gauge add up to the measured total in a simple bucket (evaporation is prevented with an appropriate substance such as mineral oil)? Drip from overhanging foliage and trees can augment precipitation totals.

D.3.2.3. Precipitation (frozen): Calm locations or shielding are a must. Undercatch for rain is only about 5 percent, but with winds of only 2–4 m/s, gauges may catch only 30–70 percent of the actual snow falling depending on density of the flakes. To catch 100 percent of the snow, the standard configuration for shielding is employed by the CRN (Climate Reference Network): the DFIR (Double-Fence Intercomparison Reference) shield with 2.4-m (8-ft.) vertical, wooden slatted fences in two concentric octagons with diameters of 8 m and 4 m (26 ft and 13 ft, respectively) and an inner Alter shield (flapping vanes). Numerous tests have shown this is the only way to achieve complete catch of snowfall (e.g., Yang et al. 1998; 2001). The DFIR shield is large and bulky; it is recommended that all precipitation gauges have at least Alter shields on them.

Near oceans, much snow is heavy and falls more vertically. In colder locations or storms, light flakes frequently will fly in and then out of the gauge. Clearings in forests are usually excellent sites. Snow blowing from trees that are too close can augment actual precipitation totals. Artificial shielding (vanes, etc.) placed around gauges in snowy locales always should be used if accurate totals are desired. Moving parts tend to freeze up. Capping of gauges during heavy snowfall events is a common occurrence. When the cap becomes pointed, snow falls off to the ground and is not recorded. Caps and plugs often will not fall into the tube until hours, days, or even weeks have passed, typically during an extended period of freezing temperature or above or when sunlight finally occurs. Liquid-based measurements (e.g., SNOTEL "rocket" gauges) do not have the resolution (usually 0.3 cm [0.1 in.] rather than 0.03 cm [0.01 in.]) that tipping bucket and other gauges have but are known to be reasonably accurate in very snowy climates. Light snowfall events might not be recorded until enough of them add up to the next reporting increment. More expensive gauges like Geonors can be considered and could do quite well in snowy settings; however, they need to be emptied every 40 cm (15 in.) or so (capacity of 51 cm [20 in.]) until the new 91-cm (36-in.) capacity gauge is offered for sale. Recently, the NWS has been trying out the new (and very expensive) Ott all-weather gauge. Riming can be an issue in windy foggy environments below freezing. Rime, dew, and other forms of atmospheric condensation are not real precipitation, since they are caused by the gauge.

D.3.2.4. Snow Depth: Windswept areas tend to be blown clear of snow. Conversely, certain types of vegetation can act as a snow fence and cause artificial drifts. However, some amount of vegetation in the vicinity generally can help slow down the wind. The two most common types of snow-depth gauges are the Judd Snow Depth Sensor, produced by Judd Communications, and the snow depth gauge produced by Campbell Scientific, Inc. Opinions vary on which one is better. These gauges use ultrasound and look downward in a cone about 22 degrees in diameter. The ground should be relatively clear of vegetation and maintained in a manner so that the zero point on the calibration scale does not change.

D.3.2.5. Snow Water Equivalent: This is determined by the weight of snow on fluid-filled pads about the size of a desktop set up sometimes in groups of four or in larger hexagons several meters in diameter. These pads require flat ground some distance from nearby sources of windblown snow and shielding that is "just right": not too close to the shielding to act as a kind of snow fence and not too far from the shielding so that blowing and drifting become a factor. Generally, these pads require fluids that possess antifreeze-like properties, as well as handling and replacement protocols.

D.3.2.6. Wind: Open exposures are needed for wind measurements. Small prominences or benches without blockage from certain sectors are preferred. A typical rule for trees is to site stations back 10 tree-heights from all tree obstructions. Sites in long, narrow valleys can obviously only exhibit two main wind directions. Gently rounded eminences are more favored. Any kind of topographic steering should be avoided to the extent possible. Avoiding major mountain chains or single isolated mountains or ridges is usually a favorable approach, if there is a choice. Sustained wind speed and the highest gusts (1-second) should be recorded. Averaging methodologies for both sustained winds and gusts can affect climate trends and should be recorded as metadata with all changes noted. Vegetation growth affects the vertical wind profile, and growth over a few years can lead to changes in mean wind speed even if the "real" wind does not change, so vegetation near the site (perhaps out to 50 m) should be maintained in a quasi-permanent status (same height and spatial distribution). Wind devices can rime up and freeze or spin out of balance. In severely rimed or windy climates, rugged anemometers, such as those made by Taylor, are worth considering. These anemometers are expensive but durable and can withstand substantial abuse. In exposed locations, personnel should plan for winds to be at least 50 m/s and be able to measure these wind speeds. At a minimum, anemometers should be rated to 75 m/s.

D.3.2.7. Humidity: Humidity is a relatively straightforward climate element. Close proximity to lakes or other water features can affect readings. Humidity readings typically are less accurate near 100 percent and at low humidities in cold weather.

D.3.2.8. Solar Radiation: A site with an unobstructed horizon obviously is the most desirable. This generally implies a flat plateau or summit. However, in most locations trees or mountains will obstruct the sun for part of the day.

D.3.2.9. Soil Temperature: It is desirable to measure soil temperature at locations where soil is present. If soil temperature is recorded at only a single depth, the most preferred depth is 10 cm. Other common depths include 25 cm, 50 cm, 2 cm, and 100 cm. Biological activity in the soil will be proportional to temperature with important threshold effects occurring near freezing.

D.3.2.10. Soil Moisture: Soil-moisture gauges are somewhat temperamental and require care to install. The soil should be characterized by a soil expert during installation of the gauge. The readings may require a certain level of experience to interpret correctly. If accurate, readings of soil moisture are especially useful.

D.3.2.11. Distributed Observations: It can be seen readily that compromises must be struck among the considerations described in the preceding paragraphs because some are mutually exclusive.

How large can a "site" be? Generally, the equipment footprint should be kept as small as practical with all components placed next to each other (within less than 10–20 m or so). Readings from one instrument frequently are used to aid in interpreting readings from the remaining instruments.

What is a tolerable degree of separation? Some consideration may be given to locating a precipitation gauge or snow pillow among protective vegetation, while the associated temperature, wind, and humidity readings would be collected more effectively in an open and exposed location within 20–50 m. Ideally, it is advantageous to know the wind measurement precisely at the precipitation gauge, but a compromise involving a short split, and in effect a "distributed observation," could be considered. There are no definitive rules governing this decision, but it is suggested that the site footprint be kept within approximately 50 m. There also are constraints imposed by engineering and electrical factors that affect cable lengths, signal strength, and line noise; therefore, the shorter the cable the better. Practical issues include the need to trench a channel to outlying instruments or to allow lines to lie atop the ground and associated problems with animals, humans, weathering, etc. Separating a precipitation gauge up to 100 m or so from an instrument mast may be an acceptable compromise if other factors are not limiting.

D.3.2.12. Instrument Replacement Schedules: Instruments slowly degrade, and a plan for replacing them with new, refurbished, or recalibrated instruments should be in place. After approximately five years, a systematic change-out procedure should result in replacing most sensors in a network. Certain parts, such as solar radiation sensors, are candidates for annual calibration or change-out. Anemometers tend to degrade as bearings erode or electrical contacts become uneven. Noisy bearings are an indication, and a stethoscope might aid in hearing such noises. Increased internal friction affects the threshold starting speed; once spinning, they tend to function properly. Increases in starting threshold speeds can lead to more zero-wind measurements and thus reduce the reported mean wind speed with no real change in wind properties. A field calibration kit should be developed and taken on all site visits, routine or otherwise. Rain gauges can be tested with drip testers during field visits. Protective conduit and tight water seals can prevent abrasion and moisture problems with the equipment, although seals can keep moisture in as well as out. Bulletproof casings sometimes are employed in remote settings. A supply of spare parts, at least one of each and more for less-expensive or more-delicate sensors, should be maintained to allow replacement of worn or nonfunctional instruments during field visits. In addition, this approach allows instruments to be calibrated in the relative convenience of the operational home—the larger the network, the greater the need for a parts depot.

D.3.3. Long-Term Comparability and Consistency

D.3.3.1. Consistency: The emphasis here is to hold biases constant. Every site has biases, problems, and idiosyncrasies of one sort or another. The best rule to follow is simply to try to keep biases constant through time. Since the goal is to track climate through time, keeping sensors, methodologies, and exposure constant will ensure that only true climate change is being measured. This means leaving the site in its original state or performing maintenance to keep it that way. Once a site is installed, the goal should be to never move the site even by a few meters or to allow significant changes to occur within 100 m for the next several decades.

Sites in or near rock outcroppings likely will experience less vegetative disturbance or growth through the years and will not usually retain moisture, a factor that could speed corrosion. Sites that will remain locally similar for some time are usually preferable. However, in some cases the intent of a station might be to record the local climate effects of changes within a small-scale system (for example, glacier, recently burned area, or scene of some other disturbance) that is subject to a regional climate influence. In this example, the local changes might be much larger than the regional changes.

D.3.3.2. Metadata: Since the climate of every site is affected by features in the immediate vicinity, it is vital to record this information over time and to update the record repeatedly at each service visit. Distances, angles, heights of vegetation, fine-scale topography, condition of instruments, shielding discoloration, and other factors from within a meter to several kilometers should be noted. Systematic photography should be undertaken and updated at least once every one–two years.

Photographic documentation should be taken at each site in a standard manner and repeated every two–three years. Guidelines for methodology were developed by Redmond (2004) as a result of experience with the NOAA CRN and can be found on the WRCC NPS Web pages at http://www.wrcc.dri.edu/nps and at ftp://ftp.wrcc.dri.edu/nps/photodocumentation.pdf.

The main purpose for climate stations is to *track climatic conditions through time*. Anything that affects the interpretation of records through time must to be noted and recorded for posterity. The important factors should be clear to a person who has never visited the site, no matter how long ago the site was installed.

In regions with significant, climatic transition zones, transects are an efficient way to span several climates and make use of available resources. Discussions on this topic at greater detail can be found in Redmond and Simeral (2004) and in Redmond et al. (2005).

D.4. Literature Cited

American Association of State Climatologists. 1985. Heights and exposure standards for sensors on automated weather stations. The State Climatologist **9**.

Brock, F. V., K. C. Crawford, R. L. Elliott, G. W. Cuperus, S. J. Stadler, H. L. Johnson and M. D. Eilts. 1995. The Oklahoma Mesonet: A technical overview. Journal of Atmospheric and Oceanic Technology **12**:5-19.

Daly, C., R. P. Neilson, and D. L. Phillips. 1994. A statistical-topographic model for mapping climatological precipitation over mountainous terrain. Journal of Applied Meteorology **33**:140-158.

Daly, C., W. P. Gibson, G. H. Taylor, G. L. Johnson, and P. Pasteris. 2002. A knowledge-based approach to the statistical mapping of climate. Climate Research **22**:99-113.

Doggett, M., C. Daly, J. Smith, W. Gibson, G. Taylor, G. Johnson, and P. Pasteris. 2004. High-resolution 1971-2000 mean monthly temperature maps for the western United States. Fourteenth AMS Conf. on Applied Climatology, 84th AMS Annual Meeting. Seattle, WA, American Meteorological Society, Boston, MA, January 2004, Paper 4.3, CD-ROM.

Geiger, R., R. H. Aron, and P. E. Todhunter. 2003. The Climate Near the Ground. 6th edition. Rowman & Littlefield Publishers, Inc., New York.

Gibson, W. P., C. Daly, T. Kittel, D. Nychka, C. Johns, N. Rosenbloom, A. McNab, and G. Taylor. 2002. Development of a 103-year high-resolution climate data set for the conterminous United States. Thirteenth AMS Conf. on Applied Climatology. Portland, OR, American Meteorological Society, Boston, MA, May 2002:181-183.

Goodison, B. E., P. Y. T. Louie, and D. Yang. 1998. WMO solid precipitation measurement intercomparison final report. WMO TD 982, World Meteorological Organization, Geneva, Switzerland.

National Research Council. 1998. Future of the National Weather Service Cooperative Weather Network. National Academies Press, Washington, D.C.

National Research Council. 2001. A Climate Services Vision: First Steps Toward the Future. National Academies Press, Washington, D.C.

Redmond, K. T. 1992. Effects of observation time on interpretation of climatic time series - A need for consistency. Eighth Annual Pacific Climate (PACLIM) Workshop. Pacific Grove, CA, March 1991:141-150.

Redmond, K. T. 2004. Photographic documentation of long-term climate stations. Available from ftp://ftp.wrcc.dri.edu/nps/photodocumentation.pdf. (accessed 15 August 2004)

Redmond, K. T. and D. B. Simeral. 2004. Climate monitoring comments: Central Alaska Network Inventory and Monitoring Program. Available from ftp://ftp.wrcc.dri.edu/nps/alaska/cakn/npscakncomments040406.pdf. (accessed 6 April 2004)

Redmond, K. T., D. B. Simeral, and G. D. McCurdy. 2005. Climate monitoring for southwest Alaska national parks: network design and site selection. Report 05-01. Western Regional Climate Center, Reno, Nevada.

Redmond, K. T., and G. D. McCurdy. 2005. Channel Islands National Park: Design considerations for weather and climate monitoring. Report 05-02. Western Regional Climate Center, Reno, Nevada.

Sevruk, B., and W. R. Hamon. 1984. International comparison of national precipitation gauges with a reference pit gauge. Instruments and Observing Methods, Report No 17, WMO/TD – 38, World Meteorological Organization, Geneva, Switzerland.

Simpson, J. J., Hufford, G. L., C. Daly, J. S. Berg, and M. D. Fleming. 2005. Comparing maps of mean monthly surface temperature and precipitation for Alaska and adjacent areas of Canada produced by two different methods. Arctic **58**:137-161.

Whiteman, C. D. 2000. Mountain Meteorology: Fundamentals and Applications. Oxford University Press, Oxford, UK.

Wilson, E. O. 1998. Consilience: The Unity of Knowledge. Knopf, New York.

World Meteorological Organization. 1983. Guide to meteorological instruments and methods of observation, No. 8, 5th edition, World Meteorological Organization, Geneva Switzerland.

World Meteorological Organization. 2005. Organization and planning of intercomparisons of rainfall intensity gauges. World Meteorological Organization, Geneva Switzerland.

Yang, D., B. E. Goodison, J. R. Metcalfe, V. S. Golubev, R. Bates, T. Pangburn, and C. Hanson. 1998. Accuracy of NWS 8" standard nonrecording precipitation gauge: results and application of WMO intercomparison. Journal of Atmospheric and Oceanic Technology **15**:54-68.

Yang, D., B. E. Goodison, J. R. Metcalfe, P. Louie, E. Elomaa, C. Hanson, V. Bolubev, T. Gunther, J. Milkovic, and M. Lapin. 2001. Compatibility evaluation of national precipitation gauge measurements. Journal of Geophysical Research **106**:1481-1491.

Appendix E. Master metadata field list

Field Name	Field Type	Field Description
begin_date	date	Effective beginning date for a record.
begin_date_flag	char(2)	Flag describing the known accuracy of the begin date for a station.
best_elevation	float(4)	Best known elevation for a station (in feet).
clim_div_code	char(2)	Foreign key defining climate division code (primary in table: clim_div).
clim_div_key	int2	Foreign key defining climate division for a station (primary in table: clim_div.
clim_div_name	varchar(30)	English name for a climate division.
controller_info	varchar(50)	Person or organization who maintains the identifier system for a given weather or climate network.
country_key	int2	Foreign key defining country where a station resides (primary in table: none).
county_key	int2	Foreign key defining county where a station resides (primary in table: county).
county_name	varchar(31)	English name for a county.
description	text	Any description pertaining to the particular table.
end_date	date	Last effective date for a record.
end_date_flag	char(2)	Flag describing the known accuracy of station end date.
fips_country_code	char(2)	FIPS (federal information processing standards) country code.
fips_state_abbr	char(2)	FIPS state abbreviation for a station.
fips_state_code	char(2)	FIPS state code for a station.
history_flag	char(2)	Describes temporal significance of an individual record among others from the same station.
id_type_key	int2	Foreign key defining the id_type for a station (usually defined in code).
last_updated	date	Date of last update for a record.
latitude	float(8)	Latitude value.
longitude	float(8)	Longitude value.
name_type_key	int2	"3": COOP station name, "2": best station name.
name	varchar(30)	Station name as known at date of last update entry.
ncdc_state_code	char(2)	NCDC, two-character code identifying U.S. state.
network_code	char(8)	Eight-character abbreviation code identifying a network.
network_key	int2	Foreign key defining the network for a station (primary in table: network).
network_station_id	int4	Identifier for a station in the associated network, which is defined by id_type_key.
remark	varchar(254)	Additional information for a record.
src_quality_code	char(2)	Code describing the data quality for the data source.
state_key	int2	Foreign key defining the U.S. state where a station resides (primary in table: state).
state_name	varchar(30)	English name for a state.
station_alt_name	varchar(30)	Other English names for a station.
station_best_name	varchar(30)	Best, most well-known English name for a station.
time_zone	float4	Time zone where a station resides.
ucan_station_id	int4	Unique station identifier for every station in ACIS.
unit_key	int2	Integer value representing a unit of measure.

Field Name	Field Type	Field Description
updated_by	char(8)	Person who last updated a record.
var_major_id	int2	Defines major climate variable.
var_minor_id	int2	Defines data source within a var_major_id.
zipcode	char(5)	Zipcode where a latitude/longitude point resides.
nps_netcode	char(4)	Network four-character identifier.
nps_netname	varchar(128)	Displayed English name for a network.
parkcode	char(4)	Park four-character identifier.
parkname	varchar(128)	Displayed English name for a park/
im_network	char(4)	NPS I&M network where park belongs (a net code)/
station_id	varchar(16)	Station identifier.
station_id_type	varchar(16)	Type of station identifier.
network.subnetwork.id	varchar(16)	Identifier of a sub-network in associated network.
subnetwork_key	int2	Foreign key defining sub-network for a station.
subnetwork_name	varchar(30)	English name for a sub-network.
slope	integer	Terrain slope at the location.
aspect	integer	Terrain aspect at the station.
gps	char(1)	Indicator of latitude/longitude recorded via GPS.
site_description	text(0)	Physical description of site.
route_directions	text(0)	Driving route or site access directions.
station_photo_id	integer	Unique identifier associating a group of photos to a station. Group of photos all taken on same date.
photo_id	char(30)	Unique identifier for a photo.
photo_date	datetime	Date photograph taken.
photographer	varchar(64)	Name of photographer.
maintenance_date	datetime	Date of station maintenance visit.
contact_key	Integer	Unique identifier associating contact information to a station.
full_name	varchar(64)	Full name of contact person.
organization	varchar(64)	Organization of contact person.
contact_type	varchar(32)	Type of contact person (operator, administrator, etc.)
position_title	varchar(32)	Title of contact person.
address	varchar(32)	Address for contact person.
city	varchar(32)	City for contact person.
state	varchar(2)	State for contact person.
zip_code	char(10)	Zipcode for contact person.
country	varchar(32)	Country for contact person.
email	varchar(64)	E-mail for contact person.
work_phone	varchar(16)	Work phone for contact person.
contact_notes	text(254)	Other details regarding contact person.
equipment_type	char(30)	Sensor measurement type; i.e., wind speed, air temperature, etc.
eq_manufacturer	char(30)	Manufacturer of equipment.
eq_model	char(20)	Model number of equipment.
serial_num	char(20)	Serial number of equipment.
eq_description	varchar(254)	Description of equipment.
install_date	datetime	Installation date of equipment.
remove_date	datetime	Removal date of equipment.
ref_height	integer	Sensor displacement height from surface.
sampling_interval	varchar(10)	Frequency of sensor measurement.

Appendix F. Electronic supplements

F.1. ACIS metadata file for weather and climate stations associated with the SFAN:
http://www.wrcc.dri.edu/nps/pub/SFAN/metadata/SFAN_from_ACIS.tar.gz.

Appendix G. Descriptions of weather/climate monitoring networks

G.1. California Air Resources Board (CARB) Network

- Purpose of network: provide meteorological data in support of air resource monitoring efforts in California.
- Data websites: http://www.met.utah.edu/jhorel/html/mesonet and http://www.arb.ca.gov.
- Measured weather/climate elements:
  - o Air temperature.
  - o Relative humidity.
  - o Precipitation.
  - o Wind speed and direction.
- Sampling frequency: hourly.
- Reporting frequency: hourly.
- Estimated station cost: unknown.
- Network strengths:
  - o Data are in near-real-time.
  - o Extensive coverage in California.
- Network weaknesses:
  - o Limited number of meteorological elements.

Meteorological measurements are taken at CARB sites in support of their overall mission of promoting and protecting public health, welfare and ecological resources in California through the reduction of air pollutants, while accounting for economical effects of such measures.

G.2. Clean Air Status and Trends Network (CASTNet)

- Purpose of network: provide information for evaluating the effectiveness of national emission-control strategies.
- Primary management agency: EPA.
- Data website: http://epa.gov/castnet/.
- Measured weather/climate elements:
  - o Air temperature.
  - o Precipitation.
  - o Relative humidity.
  - o Wind speed.
  - o Wind direction.
  - o Wind gust.
  - o Gust direction.
  - o Solar radiation.
  - o Soil moisture and temperature.
- Sampling frequency: hourly.
- Reporting frequency: hourly.
- Estimated station cost: $13000.
- Network strengths:

o High-quality data.
o Sites are well maintained.
  • Network weaknesses:
    o Density of station coverage is low.
    o Shorter periods of record for western U.S.

The CASTNet network is primarily is an air-quality-monitoring network managed by the EPA. The elements shown here are intended to support interpretation of measured air-quality parameters such as ozone, nitrates, sulfides, etc., which also are measured at CASTNet sites.

G.3. California Irrigation Management Information System (CIMIS)

  • Purpose of network: provide meteorological data to assist in irrigation activities and other water resource management issues for California agricultural interests.
  • Primary management agencies: California Department of Water Resources.
  • Data website: http://www.cimis.water.ca.gov/cimis/data.jsp.
  • Measured weather/climate elements:
    o Air temperature.
    o Precipitation.
    o Relative humidity.
    o Wind speed and direction.
    o Solar radiation.
    o Soil temperature and moisture (some sites).
  • Sampling frequency: hourly.
  • Reporting frequency: hourly.
  • Estimated station cost: unknown.
  • Network strengths:
    o Near-real-time.
    o Sites are generally well-maintained.
    o Data access.
  • Network weaknesses:
    o Somewhat limited number of meteorological elements.
    o Coverage limited to California.

The California Irrigation Management Information System (CIMIS), operated through the California Department of Water Resources, is a network of over 120 automated weather stations in the state of California. CIMIS stations are used to assist irrigators in managing their water resources efficiently.

G.4. NWS Cooperative Observer Program (COOP)

  • Purpose of network:
    o Provide observational, meteorological data required to define U.S. climate and help measure long-term climate changes.
    o Provide observational, meteorological data in near real-time to support forecasting and warning mechanisms and other public service programs of the NWS.
  • Primary management agency: NOAA (NWS).

- Data website: data are available from the NCDC (http://www.ncdc.noaa.gov), RCCs (e.g., WRCC, http://www.wrcc.dri.edu), and state climate offices.
- Measured weather/climate elements:
  o Maximum, minimum, and observation-time temperature.
  o Precipitation, snowfall, snow depth.
  o Pan evaporation (some stations).
- Sampling frequency: daily.
- Reporting frequency: daily or monthly (station-dependent).
- Estimated station cost: $2000 with maintenance costs of $500–900/year.
- Network strengths:
  o Decade–century records at most sites.
  o Widespread national coverage (thousands of stations).
  o Excellent data quality when well maintained.
  o Relatively inexpensive; highly cost effective.
  o Manual measurements; not automated.
- Network weaknesses:
  o Uneven exposures; many are not well-maintained.
  o Dependence on schedules for volunteer observers.
  o Slow entry of data from many stations into national archives.
  o Data subject to observational methodology; not always documented.
  o Manual measurements; not automated and not hourly.

The COOP network has long served as the main climate observation network in the U.S. Readings are usually made by volunteers using equipment supplied, installed, and maintained by the federal government. The observer in effect acts as a host for the data-gathering activities and supplies the labor; this is truly a "cooperative" effort. The SAO sites often are considered to be part of the cooperative network as well if they collect the previously mentioned types of weather/climate observations. Typical observation days are morning to morning, evening to evening, or midnight to midnight. By convention, observations are ascribed to the date the instrument was reset at the end of the observational period. For this reason, midnight observations represent the end of a day. The Historical Climate Network is a subset of the cooperative network but contains longer and more complete records.

G.5. Citizen Weather Observer Program (CWOP)

- Purpose of network: collect observations from private citizens and make these data available for homeland security and other weather applications, providing constant feedback to the observers to maintain high data quality.
- Primary management agency: NOAA MADIS program.
- Data Website: http://www.wxqa.com.
- Measured weather/climate elements:
  o Air temperature.
  o Dewpoint temperature.
  o Precipitation.
  o Wind speed and direction.
  o Barometric pressure.

- Sampling frequency: 15 minutes or less.
- Reporting frequency: 15 minutes.
- Estimated station cost: unknown.
- Network strengths:
  o Active partnership between public agencies and private citizens.
  o Large number of participant sites.
  o Regular communications between data providers and users, encouraging higher data quality.
- Network weaknesses:
  o Variable instrumentation platforms.
  o Metadata are sometimes limited.

The CWOP network is a public-private partnership with U.S. citizens and various agencies including NOAA, NASA (National Aeronautics and Space Administration), and various universities. There are over 4500 registered sites worldwide, with close to 3000 of these sites located in North America.

G.6. Desert Research Institute (DRI) Network

- Purpose of network: sample weather and climate in various desert and mountain locations in support of ongoing research activities at WRCC and Desert Research Institute.
- Primary management agencies: WRCC and Desert Research Institute.
- Data website: http://www.wrcc.dri.edu.
- Measured weather/climate elements:
  o Air temperature.
  o Precipitation.
  o Relative humidity and dewpoint temperature.
  o Wind speed and direction.
  o Barometric pressure.
  o Solar radiation.
- Sampling frequency: every 3 seconds.
- Reporting frequency: every 10 minutes.
- Estimated station cost: $10000, with maintenance costs of about $2000 per year.
- Network strengths:
  o High-quality data and metadata.
  o Sites are well-maintained.
  o Data are in near-real-time.
- Network weaknesses:
  o Network has relatively small geographical extent (Nevada and its immediate surroundings).

The Desert Research Institute (DRI) operates this network of automated weather stations, located primarily in California and Western Nevada. Many of these stations are located in remote mountain and desert locations and provide data that are often used in support of various mountain- and desert-based environmental studies in the region.

G.7. NPS Gaseous Pollutant Monitoring Program (GPMP)

- Purpose of network: measurement of ozone and related meteorological elements.
- Primary management agency: NPS.
- Data website: http://www2.nature.nps.gov/air/monitoring.
- Measured weather/climate elements:
  o Air temperature.
  o Relative humidity.
  o Precipitation.
  o Wind speed and direction.
  o Solar radiation.
  o Surface wetness.
- Sampling frequency: continuous.
- Reporting frequency: hourly.
- Estimated station cost: unknown.
- Network strengths:
  o Stations are located within NPS park units.
  o Data quality is excellent, with high data standards.
  o Provides unique measurements that are not available elsewhere.
  o Records are up to 2 decades in length.
  o Site maintenance is excellent.
  o Thermometers are aspirated.
- Network weaknesses:
  o Not easy to download the entire data set or to ingest live data.
  o Period of record is short compared to other automated networks.
  o Station spacing and coverage: station installation is episodic, driven by opportunistic situations.

The NPS web site indicates that there are 33 sites with continuous ozone analysis run by NPS, with records from a few to about 16-17 years. Of these stations, 12 are labeled as GPMP sites and the rest are labeled as CASTNet sites. All of these have standard meteorological measurements, including a 10-m mast. Another nine GPMP sites are located within NPS units but run by cooperating agencies. A number of other sites (1-2 dozen) ran for differing periods in the past, generally less than 5-10 years.

G.8. NOAA Ground-Based GPS Meteorology (GPS-MET) Network

- Purpose of network:
  o Measure atmospheric water vapor using ground-based GPS receivers.
  o Facilitate use of these data operational and in other research and applications.
  o Provides data for weather forecasting, atmospheric modeling and prediction, climate monitoring, calibrating and validation other observing systems including radiosondes and satellites, and research.
- Primary management agency: NOAA Earth System Research Laboratory.
- Data website: http://gpsmet.noaa.gov/jsp/index.jsp.
- Measurements:
  o Dual frequency carrier phase measurements every 30 seconds.

- Ancillary weather/climate observations:
  - o Air temperature.
  - o Relative humidity.
  - o Barometric pressure.
- Reporting frequency: currently 30 min.
- Estimated station cost: $0-$10000, depending on approach. Data from dual frequency GPS receivers installed for conventional applications (e.g., high accuracy surveying) can be used without modification.
- Network strengths:
  - o Frequent, high-quality measurements.
  - o High reliability.
  - o All-weather operability.
  - o Many uses.
  - o Highly leveraged.
  - o Requires no calibration.
  - o Measurement accuracy improves with time.
- Network weakness:
  - o Point measurement.
  - o Provides no direct information about the vertical distribution of water vapor.

The GPS-MET network is the first network of its kind dedicated to GPS meteorology (see Duan et al. 1996). The GPS-MET network was developed in response to the need for improved moisture observations to support weather forecasting, climate monitoring, and other research activities. GPS-MET is a collaboration between NOAA and several other governmental and university organizations and institutions.

GPS meteorology utilizes the radio signals broadcast by the satellite Global Positioning System for atmospheric remote sensing. GPS meteorology applications have evolved along two paths: ground-based (Bevis et al. 1992) and space-based (Yuan et al. 1993). Both applications make the same fundamental measurement (the apparent delay in the arrival of radio signals caused by changes in the radio-refractivity of the atmosphere along the paths of the radio signals) but they do so from different perspectives.

In ground-based GPS meteorology, a GPS receiver and antenna are placed at a fixed location on the ground and the signals from all GPS satellites in view are continuously recorded. From this information, the exact position of the GPS antenna can be determined over time with high (millimeter-level) accuracy. Subsequent measurements of the antenna position are compared with the known position, and the differences can be attributed to changes in the temperature, pressure and water vapor in the atmosphere above the antenna. By making continuous measurements of temperature and pressure at the site, the total amount of water vapor in the atmosphere at this location can be estimated with high accuracy under all weather conditions. For more information on ground based GPS meteorology the reader is referred to http://gpsmet.noaa.gov.

In space-based GPS meteorology, GPS receivers and antennas are placed on satellites in Low Earth Orbit (LEO), and the signals transmitted by a GPS satellite are continuously recorded as a

GPS satellite "rises" or "sets" behind the limb of the Earth. This process is called an occultation or a limb sounding. The GPS radio signals bend more as they encounter a thicker atmosphere and the bending (which causes an apparent increase in the length of the path of the radio signal) can be attributed to changes in temperature, pressure and water vapor along the path of the radio signal through the atmosphere that is nominally about 300 km long. The location of an occultation depends on the relative geometries of the GPS satellites in Mid Earth Orbit and the satellites in LEO. As a consequence, information about the vertical temperature, pressure and moisture structure of the Earth's atmosphere as a whole can be estimated with high accuracy, but not at any one particular place over time. The main difference between ground and space-based GPS meteorology is one of geometry. A space-based measurement can be thought of as a ground-based measurement turned on its side. For more information on space based GPS meteorology, the reader is referred to http://www.cosmic.ucar.edu/gpsmet/.

G.9. National Atmospheric Deposition Program (NADP)

- Purpose of network: measurement of precipitation chemistry and atmospheric deposition.
- Primary management agencies: USDA, but multiple collaborators.
- Data website: http://nadp.sws.uiuc.edu.
- Measured weather/climate elements:
  o Precipitation.
- Sampling frequency: daily.
- Reporting frequency: daily.
- Estimated station cost: unknown.
- Network strengths:
  o Data quality is excellent, with high data standards.
  o Site maintenance is excellent.
- Network weaknesses:
  o A very limited number of climate parameters are measured.

Stations within the NADP network monitor primarily wet deposition through precipitation chemistry at selected sites around the U.S. and its territories. The network is a collaborative effort among several agencies including USGS and USDA. Precipitation is the primary climate parameter measured at NADP sites.

G.10. Remote Automated Weather Station (RAWS) Network

- Purpose of network: provide near-real-time (hourly or near hourly) measurements of meteorological variables for use in fire weather forecasts and climatology. Data from RAWS also are used for natural resource management, flood forecasting, natural hazard management, and air-quality monitoring.
- Primary management agency: WRCC, National Interagency Fire Center.
- Data website: http://www.raws.dri.edu/index.html.
- Measured weather/climate elements:
  o Air temperature.
  o Precipitation.
  o Relative humidity.
  o Wind speed.

o Wind direction.
o Wind gust.
o Gust direction.
o Solar radiation.
o Soil moisture and temperature.
- Sampling frequency: 1 or 10 minutes, element-dependent.
- Reporting frequency: generally hourly. Some stations report every 15 or 30 minutes.
- Estimated station cost: $12000 with satellite telemetry ($8000 without satellite telemetry); maintenance costs are around $2000/year.
- Network strengths:
o Metadata records are usually complete.
o Sites are located in remote areas.
o Sites are generally well-maintained.
o Entire period of record available on-line.
- Network weaknesses:
o RAWS network is focused largely on fire management needs (formerly focused only on fire needs).
o Frozen precipitation is not measured reliably.
o Station operation is not always continuous.
o Data transmission is completed via one-way telemetry. Data are therefore recoverable either in real-time or not at all.

The RAWS network is used by many land-management agencies, such as the BLM, NPS, Fish and Wildlife Service, Bureau of Indian Affairs, Forest Service, and other agencies. The RAWS network was one of the first automated weather station networks to be installed in the U.S. Most gauges do not have heaters, so hydrologic measurements are of little value when temperatures dip below freezing or reach freezing after frozen precipitation events. There are approximately 1100 real-time sites in this network and about 1800 historic sites (some are decommissioned or moved). The sites can transmit data all winter but may be in deep snow in some locations. The WRCC is the archive for this network and receives station data and metadata through a special connection to the National Interagency Fire Center in Boise, Idaho.

G.11. NWS/FAA Surface Airways Observation Network (SAO)

- Purpose of network: provide near-real-time (hourly or near hourly) measurements of meteorological variables and are used both for airport operations and weather forecasting.
- Primary management agency: NOAA, FAA.
- Data website: data are available from state climate offices, RCCs (e.g., WRCC, http://www.wrcc.dri.edu), and NCDC (http://www.ncdc.noaa.gov).
- Measured weather/climate elements:
o Air temperature.
o Dewpoint and/or relative humidity.
o Wind speed.
o Wind direction.
o Wind gust.
o Gust direction.

o Barometric pressure.
o Precipitation (not at many FAA sites).
o Sky cover.
o Ceiling (cloud height).
o Visibility.
- Sampling frequency: element-dependent.
- Reporting frequency: element-dependent.
- Estimated station cost: $100000–$200000, with maintenance costs approximately $10000/year.
- Network strengths:
  o Records generally extend over several decades.
  o Consistent maintenance and station operations.
  o Data record is reasonably complete and usually high quality.
  o Hourly or sub-hourly data.
- Network weaknesses:
  o Nearly all sites are located at airports.
  o Data quality can be related to size of airport—smaller airports tend to have poorer datasets.
  o Influences from urbanization and other land-use changes.

These stations are managed by NOAA, U. S. Navy, U. S. Air Force, and FAA. These stations are located generally at major airports and military bases. The FAA stations often do not record precipitation, or they may provide precipitation records of reduced quality. Automated stations are typically ASOSs for the NWS or AWOSs for the FAA. Some sites only report episodically with observers paid per observation.

G.12. Weather For You Network (WX4U)

- Purpose of network: allow volunteer weather enthusiasts around the U.S. to observe and share weather data.
- Data website: http://www.met.utah.edu/jhorel/html/mesonet.
- Measured weather/climate elements:
  o Air temperature.
  o Relative humidity and dewpoint temperature.
  o Precipitation.
  o Wind speed and direction.
  o Wind gust and direction.
  o Barometric pressure.
- Sampling frequency: 10 minutes.
- Reporting frequency: 10 minutes.
- Estimated station cost: unknown.
- Network strengths:
  o Stations are located throughout the U.S.
  o Stations provide near-real-time observations.
- Network weaknesses:
  o Instrumentation platforms can be variable.

o Data are sometimes of questionable quality.

The WX4U network is a nationwide collection of weather stations run by local observers. Meteorological elements that are measured usually include temperature, precipitation, wind, and humidity.

NPS/SFAN/NRTR—2007/041, May 2007